Show me

Excel 5

Seta Krikorian Frantz

Read less—learn faster

Easy, illustrated steps

alpha books

File Edit Formula Format

B I A

New
Open
Links…

Save
Save As…
Save Workbook…
Delete…

Print Preview
Page Setup

International Standard Book Number: 1-56761-276-8
Library of Congress Catalog Card Number: 93-72008

95 94 93   8 7 6 5 4 3 2 1

Interpretation of the printing code: the rightmost number of the second series of numbers is the number of the book's printing. For example, a printing code of 93-1 shows that the first printing of the book occurred in 1993.

Screen reproductions in this book were created by means of the program Collage Plus from Inner Media, Inc., Hollis, NH.

Printed in the United States of America

TRADEMARKS

Publisher   *Marie Butler-Knight*
Managing Editor   *Elizabeth Keaffaber*
Product Development Manager   *Faithe Wempen*
Acquisitions Manager   *Barry Pruett*
Manuscript Editor   *San Dee Phillips*
Cover Design   *Scott Fulmer*
Interior Design   *Roger Morgan*
Index   *Jeanne Clark*
Production   *Diana Bigham-Griffin, Katy Bodenmiller, Brad Chinn, Kim Cofer, Meshell Dinn, Mark Enochs, Jenny Kucera, Beth Rago, Greg Simsic*

Special Thanks to C. Herbert Feltner for ensuring the technical accuracy of this book.

CONTENTS

Introduction 1

Part 1 Beginning Excel Tasks   11

Starting Excel...12

Understanding the Excel Workbook Screen 14

Controlling Excel's Windows 16

Choosing Menu Commands..17

Working with Dialog Boxes 19

Using Toolbars and Toolboxes 21

Getting Help 24

Opening an Existing Workbook 27

Opening a New Workbook 29

Closing a Workbook 30

Saving a Workbook 31

Searching for a Workbook 33

Quitting Excel..35

Part 2 Building a Worksheet   37

Selecting Cells 38

Entering Labels..40

Entering Values..43

Entering Dates and Times 45

Entering Formulas 47

Using Cell Ranges in Formulas.......................................50

Using Excel's Built-In Functions 52

Part 3 Editing and Formatting a Worksheet   55

Editing Cell Contents 56

Moving and Copying Cells 57

Inserting Rows and Columns 62

Deleting Rows and Columns...64

Clearing Cells 66

Finding Data in Cells...68

Replacing Data in Cells 70

Sorting Data...71

Changing Number Formats 73

Aligning Data in Cells 75

Changing Cell Widths......................................78

Changing Fonts and Text Attributes 80

Part 4 Printing a Worksheet   83

Selecting a Printer 84

Printing an Entire Worksheet or Workbook 85

Printing Part of a Worksheet 87

Using Print Preview 89

Setting Up Pages 91

Using Page Breaks 93

Adding Headers and Footers............................96

Part 5 Charting Data on a Worksheet   99

Creating a Chart with ChartWizard 100

Changing a Chart's Type 104

Giving a Chart Its Own Window 106

Editing a Chart with ChartWizard 107

Changing Values on a Chart 109

Adding a Chart Legend..................................111

Deleting Chart Elements 112

Deleting an Embedded Chart..........................113

Part 6 Automating Your Work   115

Recording a Macro 116

Running a Macro 119

Deleting a Macro 121

Assigning a Macro to a Menu 122

Installation   125

Glossary   129

Index   133

INTRODUCTION

Have you ever said to yourself, "I wish someone would just *show me* how to use Microsoft Excel?" If you have, this Show Me book is for you. In it, you won't find detailed explanations of what's going on in your computer each time you enter a command. Instead, you will see pictures that show you, step-by-step, how to perform a particular task.

This book will make you feel as though you have your very own personal trainer standing next to you, pointing at the screen, and showing you exactly what to do.

What Is Excel?

Excel is a spreadsheet program. Using Excel, you can create, manipulate, and analyze complex collections of data. These data collections are called *spreadsheets*.

Using Excel, you can easily:

- Create tables of data.

- Use formulas to calculate new information from your data.

- Produce colorful charts based on your data.

- Print out as many copies of a spreadsheet as you want.

- Save your work so that next month you can change a spreadsheet without having to recreate it.

LEARNING THE LINGO

Spreadsheet: A collection of data organized into rows and columns and displayed on your computer's screen.

Spreadsheet program: A program such as Excel used to create spreadsheets and to manipulate the spreadsheet's data in various ways in order to produce tables, charts, and reports.

A Day in the Life of a Spreadsheet

Excel calls its spreadsheets *worksheets*, and it organizes them in groups called *workbooks*. You can save, edit, and print individual worksheets or entire workbooks. As you create your worksheets in Excel, you'll follow a basic pattern:

Open an existing workbook, or create a new one. You start your work session by typing data into a new workbook or by editing an existing one.

Type in some data. This part is easy; choose the location where you want the data to appear, and then just type!

1

Review what you've typed and make changes. At this stage, you're copying or moving data from one place to another. You may even delete some data or insert new data to refine a table. The process of making changes to existing data is called *editing*.

Add pizzazz. Changing the way data looks (such as adding bold or making characters bigger) is called *formatting*.

Save your workbook. Once you're sure you have a workbook that you like, you should save it. Actually, it's best to save a workbook often during the editing phase so you can't lose any changes.

View your work before you print it. Excel gives you several ways to view your data, as you are working and right before you print your document.

Print your work. Nothing is better than holding the finished product in your own hands.

The Odds and Ends of Using a Spreadsheet Program

Before you can use Excel, you need to understand a few simple terms. Excel files are called *workbooks*. Each workbook consists of 16 *worksheets* or *documents*. A worksheet or document is comprised of many *rows* and *columns*, which intersect to form *cells*. Each cell can hold a single piece of *data*. "Data" is just a fancy computer word for information. In Excel's case, the data in a cell is usually a *value*, *text*, or a *formula*.

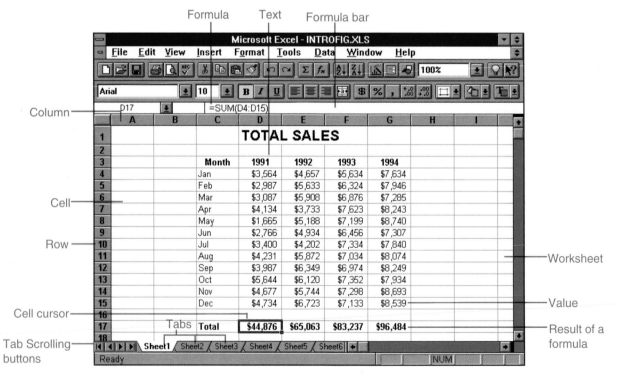

While values and text appear in a cell just as you type them, a formula appears only in the formula bar. As you can see in the figure, a cell that contains a formula shows the result of the formula. In the figure, the bottom row of cells contains four formulas, each of which sums the values in its column.

The *cell cursor* marks the place where data will be inserted. To insert data into a spreadsheet, you move the cell cursor (a black box) to the cell where you want the data stored, and then you type.

Formatting in a spreadsheet describes how data looks. Character formatting describes how a character looks. (For example, is it bold or italic?) Number formatting describes the way values appear on the screen. (For example, is the value currency?)

LEARNING THE LINGO

Workbook: Excel files are called *workbooks*. Each workbook consists of 16 worksheets or documents.

Data: Information in a computer.

Cell: The smallest part of a spreadsheet. Each cell holds a single piece of data.

Cell cursor: A black box that appears on the currently selected cell.

Formatting: The process of changing the look of a character (for example, by making it bold, underlined, and slightly bigger) or a value (for example, by adding a dollar sign or a decimal point).

Value: A number that you type into a cell.

Text: Characters that cannot be used in calculations.

Formula: Symbols and characters that calculate new values.

Cell References

In order to create formulas, you need some way to refer to cells that contain values. In Excel, as in most spreadsheet programs, you refer to a cell by typing its column letter and row number. In the figure above, for example, cell **C3** contains the text **Jan**, whereas cell **D14** contains the value **$4,734**.

Often, you need to refer to a block of cells in a formula. You can do this easily by first typing the name of the cell in the upper left corner of the block, followed by a colon (:) and the name of the cell in the lower right corner of the block. For example, to refer to all the values in the table shown in the figure, you would type **D3:G14**.

As you work with Excel, you will need to use many cell references, so it's important that you understand how to create them.

HOW TO USE THIS BOOK

Using this book is as simple as falling off your chair. Just flip to the task that you want to perform and follow the steps. You will see easy step-by-step instructions that tell you which keys to press and which commands to select. You will also see step-by-step pictures that show you what to do. Follow the steps or the pictures (or both) to complete the task.

Saving a Workbook

1 Click on the **File** menu, or press **Alt+F**.

2 Click on **Save,** or press **S**.

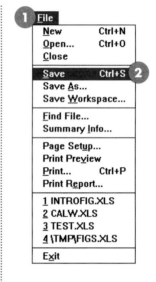

3 Type a name for the Workbook.

4 Click on **OK**, or press **Enter**.

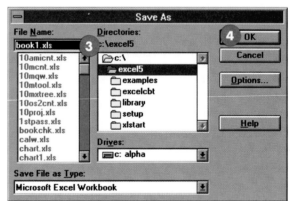

Every computer book has its own way of telling you which buttons to push and which keys to press. Here's how this book handles those formalities:

- Keys that you should press appear as they do on your keyboard; for example, press **Alt** or press **F10**. If you need to press more than one key at once, the keys are separated with plus signs. For example, if the text tells you to press **Alt+F**, hold down the **Alt** key while pressing the **F** key.

- Text that you should type is printed in **boldface type like this.**

- Some commands are activated by selecting a menu and then a command. If I tell you to "select **F**ile **N**ew," you should open the **F**ile menu and select the **N**ew command. In this book, the selection letter is printed in boldface for easy recognition.

Definitions in Plain English

In addition to the basic step-by-step approach, pages may contain Learn the Lingo definitions to help you understand key terms. These definitions are placed off to the side so you can easily skip them.

LEARNING THE LINGO

Pull-down menu: A menu that appears at the top of the screen, listing various options. The menu is not visible until you select it from the menu bar. The menu then drops down, covering a small part of the screen.

Quick Refreshers

If you need to know how to perform some other task in order to perform the current task, look for a Quick Refresher. With the Quick Refresher, you won't have to flip through the book to learn how to perform the other task; the information is right where you need it.

QUICK REFRESHER

Making dialog box selections

c:\
aol
collage
data
dos
execute
fonts

List box: Click on a list item to choose it. Use the scrollbar to view additional items.

Dri**v**es:
c: joe kraynak

Drop-down list: Click on the down arrow to the right of the list to display it. Click on the desired item.

File **N**ame:
*.exe

Text box: Click to place the I-beam in the box. Type your entry.

☐ **R**un Minimized

Check box: Click on a box to select or deselect it. (You can select more than one.)

New
○ Program **G**roup
◉ Program **I**tem

Option button: Click on a button to select it. (You can select only one button in a group.)

OK
Cancel
Help

Command button: Click on a button to execute the command. (All dialog boxes have at least two command buttons: OK to execute your selections, and Cancel to cancel the selections.)

Tips, Ideas, and Shortcuts

Throughout this book, you will encounter tips that provide important information about a task or tell you how to perform the task more quickly.

Exercises

Because most people learn by doing, exercises throughout the book give you additional practice performing a task.

Practice what you've learned about using menus by closing the open document.

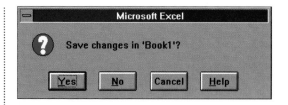

1 Click on the **File** menu or press **Alt+F**.

2 Click on **Close** or press **C**.

3 If you're asked to save your changes, click on **No** or press **N**. (We haven't done anything worth saving yet.)

TIP

Here are some keyboard shortcuts for opening and saving workbooks and for exiting the program:

Open Workbook	CTRL + O
Save Workbook	CTRL + S
Exit Excel	ALT + F4

Microsoft Excel

Save changes in 'Book1'?

Yes   No   Cancel   Help

Where Should You Start?

If this is your first encounter with computers, read the next section, "Quick Computer Tour" before reading anything else. This section explains some computer basics that you need to know in order to get your computer up and running.

Once you know the basics, you can work through this book from beginning to end or skip around from task to task, as needed. If you decide to skip around, there are several ways you can find what you're looking for:

- Use the Table of Contents at the front of this book to find a specific task you want to perform.

- Use the complete index at the back of this book to look up a specific task or topic and find the page number on which it is covered.

- Use the color coded sections to find groups of related tasks.

- Flip through the book, and look at the task titles at the top of the pages. This method works best if you know the general location of the task in the book.

- Use the inside back cover of this book to quickly find the page where a command you are looking for is covered.

QUICK COMPUTER TOUR

If this is your first time in front of a computer, the next few sections will teach you the least you need to know to get started.

Parts of a Computer

Think of a computer as a car. The system unit holds the engine that powers the computer. The monitor is like the windshield that lets you see where you're going. And the keyboard and mouse are like the steering wheel, which allow you to control the computer.

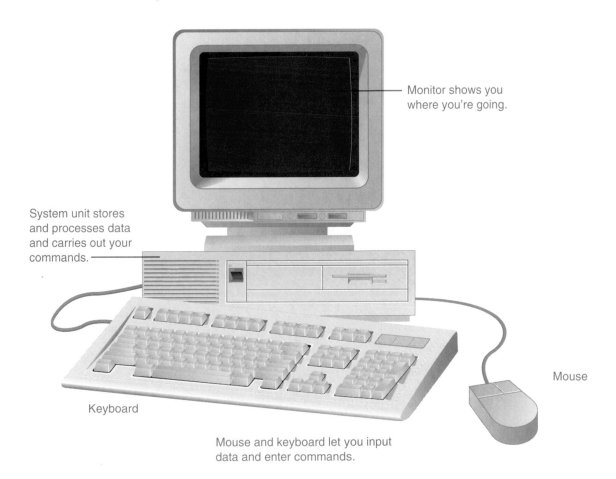

Monitor shows you where you're going.

System unit stores and processes data and carries out your commands.

Mouse

Keyboard

Mouse and keyboard let you input data and enter commands.

The System Unit

The system unit contains three basic elements: a central processing unit (CPU) that does all the "thinking" for the computer; random-access memory (RAM) that stores instructions and data while the CPU is processing it; and disk drives, which store information permanently on disks to keep the information safe. It also contains several ports (at the back), which allow you to connect other devices to it, such as a keyboard, mouse, and printer.

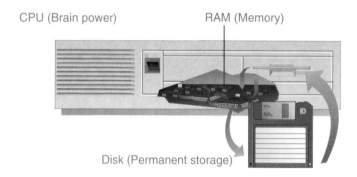

CPU (Brain power)　　　RAM (Memory)

Disk (Permanent storage)

Using a Keyboard

The keyboard is no mystery. It contains a set of alphanumeric (letter and number) keys for entering text, arrow keys for moving around on-screen, and function keys (F1, F2, and so on) for entering commands. It also has some odd keys, including Alt (Alternative), Ctrl (Control), and Esc (Escape) that perform special actions.

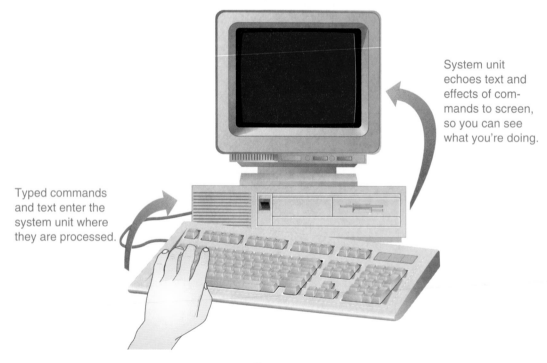

System unit echoes text and effects of commands to screen, so you can see what you're doing.

Typed commands and text enter the system unit where they are processed.

Using a Mouse

Like the keyboard, a mouse allows you to communicate with the computer. You roll the mouse around on your desk to move a mouse pointer on the screen. You can use the pointer to open menus and select other items on-screen. Here are some mouse techniques you must master:

- *Pointing*. To point, roll the mouse on your desk until the tip of the mouse pointer is on the item you want to point to.

- *Clicking*. To click on an item, point to the desired item, and then hold the mouse steady while you press and release the mouse button. Use the left mouse button unless I tell you specifically to use the right button.

- *Double-clicking*. To double-click, hold the mouse steady while you press and release the mouse button twice quickly.

- *Right-clicking*. To right-click, click using the right mouse button instead of the left button.

Understanding Disks, Directories, and Files

Whatever you type (a letter, a list of names, a tax return) is stored only in your computer's temporary memory and is erased when the electricity is turned off. To protect your work, you must save it in a file on a disk.

A file is like a folder that you might use to store a report or a letter. You name the file, so you can later find and retrieve the information it contains.

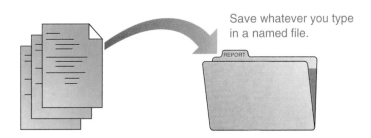

Save whatever you type in a named file.

REPORT

Files are stored on disks. Your computer probably has a hard disk inside it (called drive C) to which you can save your files. You can also save files to floppy disks, which you insert into the slots (the floppy disk drives) on the front of the computer.

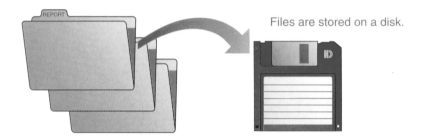

Files are stored on a disk.

To keep files organized on a disk, you can create directories on the disk. Each directory acts as a drawer in a filing cabinet, storing a group of related files. Although you can create directories on both floppy and hard disks, most people use directories only on hard disks.

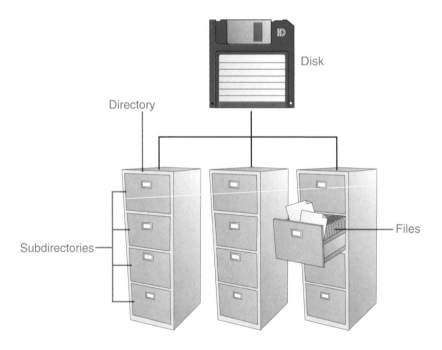

Acknowledgments

Members of the "without whom" department include Faithe Wempen, whose advice kept me on track; San Dee Phillips, who polished the words to a gleam; Herb Feltner, who made sure everything worked; and Steve Poland, who entrusted this project to me. Finally, appreciation goes to my family for watching TV without me for the weeks it took to write this book.

PART 1

Beginning Excel Tasks

This part describes basic Excel tasks that you need to know to get started. When you have finished this part, you will be able to start Excel, manipulate Excel's menus and dialog boxes, manage workbooks and worksheets, get help, and quit Excel.

- Starting Excel
- Understanding the Excel Workbook Screen
- Controlling Excel's Windows
- Choosing Menu Commands
- Working with Dialog Boxes
- Using Toolbars and Toolboxes
- Getting Help
- Opening an Existing Workbook
- Opening a New Workbook
- Closing a Workbook
- Saving a Workbook
- Searching for a Workbook
- Quitting Excel

STARTING EXCEL

Why Start Excel?

You must start Excel before you can use it. When you start Excel, the program loads into your computer's memory, and a main window appears. From this main window, you control the program, creating worksheets, charts, and other documents. Excel must be started from within Windows; if Windows is not running, type **WIN** at the DOS prompt to start it.

Before you can start Excel, it must be installed on your computer. To install Excel, refer to the section entitled "Installing Excel" found at the end of this book.

Starting Excel

1 Turn on your computer.

2 At the DOS prompt, type **WIN** and press **Enter.**

3 If the Microsoft Office group window is minimized, double-click on its **program group icon**.

You can also open the Microsoft Office group by selecting it from the Window menu.

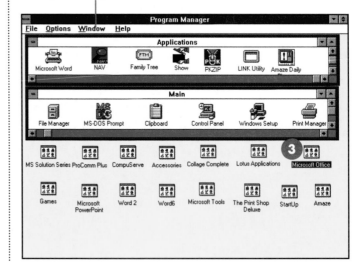

4 Double-click on the **Microsoft Excel icon**.

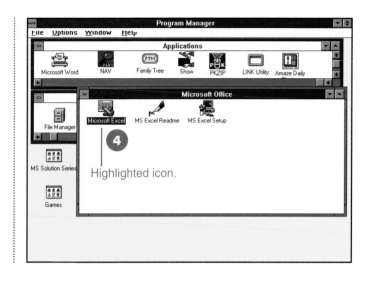

What are those Pictures?

If Windows is new to you, you may not be familiar with program groups and icons.

A *program group* icon represents a minimized program group. When you double-click it, a program group icon opens into a program group.

A *program icon* represents a program you can run. When you double-click it, the program runs.

LEARNING THE LINGO

Point: Position the mouse pointer over an object on the screen.

Click: Press and release the left mouse button.

Double-click: Press and release the left mouse button twice quickly.

Program icon: A small picture representing a program you can run. The program name usually appears under the picture.

Program group: A window containing one or more program icons.

Program group icon: A small picture representing a program group that has been minimized.

Minimized: Shrunken to the size of an icon; windows that are not in use are often minimized so they do not clutter the screen.

Beginning Excel Tasks

UNDERSTANDING THE EXCEL WORKBOOK SCREEN

What Are the Parts of the Excel Screen?

When you start Excel, it displays the screen shown in the figure below. Each section of the screen has a name and purpose that you should be aware of.

Formatting toolbar: displays button to help display cell contents with formatting.

Title bar: displays the name of the current workbook you are working on.

Menu bar: displays menu commands.

Standard toolbar: displays button that you can click with the mouse to execute commands.

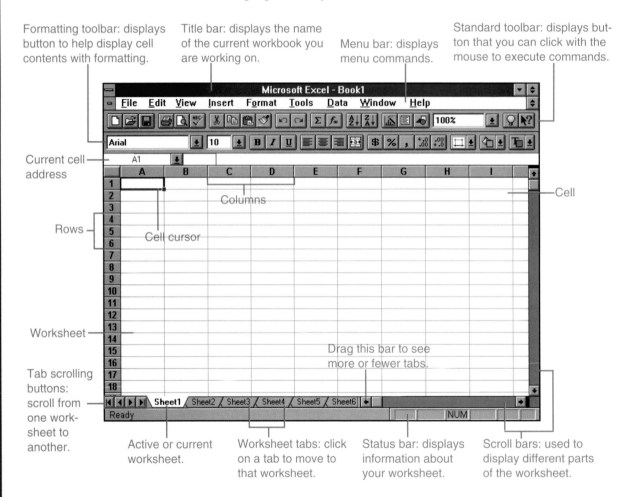

Current cell address

Columns

Cell

Rows

Cell cursor

Worksheet

Drag this bar to see more or fewer tabs.

Tab scrolling buttons: scroll from one worksheet to another.

Active or current worksheet.

Worksheet tabs: click on a tab to move to that worksheet.

Status bar: displays information about your worksheet.

Scroll bars: used to display different parts of the worksheet.

What Is the TipWizard?

Excel 5.0 offers a new feature called the TipWizard which provides you with help-ful information on how to use its powerful features. The TipWizard knows what you are currently doing and displays tips on how to do it better and faster. To turn on the TipWizard, click on the TipWizard button on the Standard toolbar. To turn it off, click on the TipWizard button again.

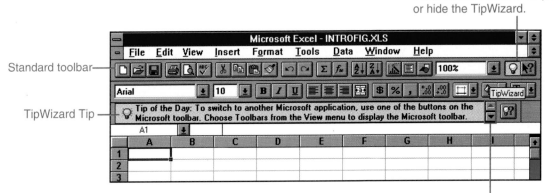

Click on this button to display or hide the TipWizard.

Standard toolbar

TipWizard Tip

Use the buttons to move to the previous or next tip.

Beginning Excel Tasks

CONTROLLING EXCEL'S WINDOWS

Why Control Windows?

Excel's windows contain many controls that you can use to manipulate the window or its contents. Using these controls, you can change the size of a window, move it around the screen, change its contents, close it, and more.

Control Menu box: double-click to close the window or Excel.

Title bar: displays the name of the program or workbook.

Minimize button: click here to reduce the window to an icon.

Restore button: click here to reduce an enlarged window to its previous size.

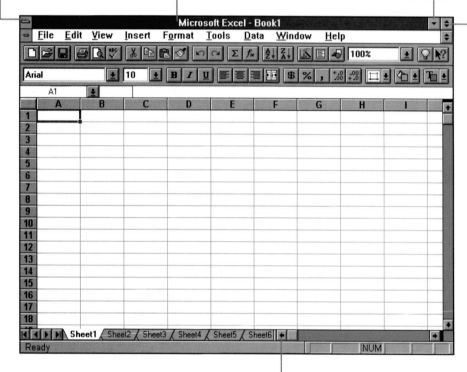

Scroll arrows: click to move row or columns up, down, left, or right one column or row.

TIP

It's Not Gone! To get a minimized window back open again, double-click on the minimized icon.

CHOOSING MENU COMMANDS

What Are Menu Commands?

All the commands needed to control Excel are located in the menus on the main menu bar. You can use your mouse or your keyboard to select any menu or menu command. When you open a menu, you'll see that it often contains shortcut keys, ellipses, and grayed-out commands. These and other menu elements are explained below:

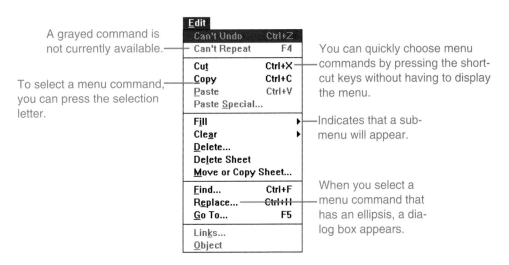

A grayed command is not currently available.

To select a menu command, you can press the selection letter.

You can quickly choose menu commands by pressing the shortcut keys without having to display the menu.

Indicates that a submenu will appear.

When you select a menu command that has an ellipsis, a dialog box appears.

Instead of typing a menu item's selection letter, you can use the up and down arrow keys to highlight the command and then press Enter.

LEARNING THE LINGO

Hot keys or Shortcut keys: Keystrokes you can use to instantly select a menu command.

Grayed-out: Grayed-out menu commands are displayed lighter than other commands and cannot be selected.

Ellipsis: An ellipsis is three dots (...). When an ellipsis follows a menu command, the command displays a dialog box when selected.

Selection letter: The underlined letter in a menu or command name.

Choosing Menu Commands

1 Click on the menu name on the menu bar, or hold down the **Alt** key, and type the selection letter (the underlined letter) in the menu name.

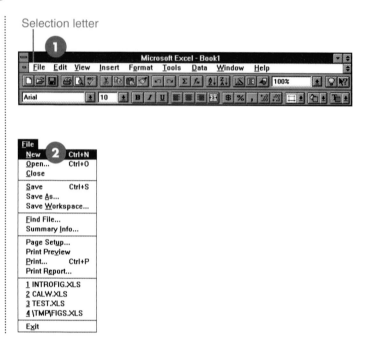

Selection letter

2 Click on the menu command you want, or type the selection letter in the command name.

If you open a menu by pressing **Alt** along with the menu's selection (underlined) letter, you can then view other menus in the menu bar by pressing your left or right arrow keys.

Exercise

Practice selecting menu commands by choosing the **O**ptions command on the **T**ools menu, which opens the Display Options dialog box.

1 Click on the Tools menu, or press **Alt+T**.

2 Click on Options, or press **O**.

3 Press **Esc** to clear the dialog box from your screen.

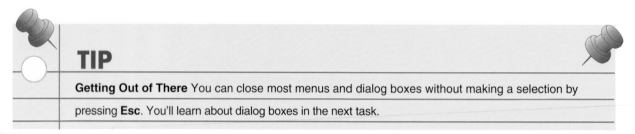

TIP

Getting Out of There You can close most menus and dialog boxes without making a selection by pressing **Esc**. You'll learn about dialog boxes in the next task.

WORKING WITH DIALOG BOXES

What Are Dialog Boxes?

Dialog boxes appear when you issue certain commands. They are small windows containing various controls and text fields with which you can provide information to Excel. Sometimes a dialog box displays only a simple question; other times a dialog box contains many lists, buttons, text-entry fields, and other controls.

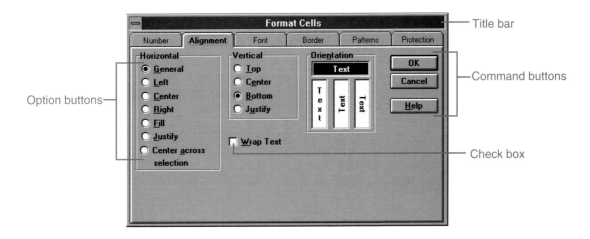

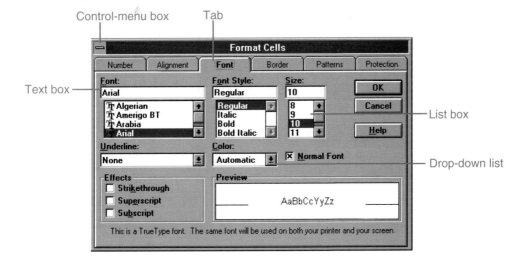

Getting out of a Dialog Box

If you want Excel to ignore any changes you've made in a dialog box, close the dialog box by clicking on the **Cancel** button, selecting **Close** in the dialog box's Control menu, or pressing **Esc**.

19

WORKING WITH DIALOG BOXES

Selecting Dialog Box Options

Command buttons: Click the button you want, or press **Tab** until a dark outline appears around the button. Then press **Enter**.

Text boxes: Click the text box to activate the blinking text cursor, or press **Tab** until it appears in the text box. Then type the required text.

Option buttons: Click on the button of your choice, or press **Tab** until a dotted box appears around the currently selected option. Then use the arrow keys to move the dotted box to the option you want.

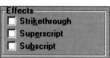

Check boxes: Click on an option to turn it on or off, or press **Tab** until a dotted box appears around an option in that area. Use the arrow keys until the dotted box moves to the desired check box, and then press the **Spacebar** to turn the option on or off.

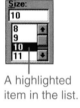

A highlighted item in the list.

List boxes: Click on the text box above the list box, and then type the item you want to select, or click on an item from the list to place it in the text box. Use the scroll bar, if needed, to reveal additional choices. Or with the keyboard, press **Tab** until the blinking text cursor appears in the text box or its current contents is highlighted. Then either type the item you want or use the arrow keys to highlight an item in the list.

Arrow button

Drop-down list box: Click on the arrow button to reveal the list, and then click on the item you want in the list. Or press **Tab** until the currently selected item is highlighted, and then press **Alt+the arrow keys** to display the available items.

Tabs: Click on a tab to reveal another window in the dialog box.

LEARNING THE LINGO

Toggle: To switch an option from on to off or from off to on.

Drag: Point to a screen object and then hold down the left mouse button while you move the mouse, dragging the pointer across the screen.

USING TOOLBARS AND TOOLBOXES

Why Use Toolbars and Toolboxes?

Many frequently used commands appear on Excel's Toolbars, where they can be selected with a quick click of your mouse. Using the Toolbars can save you from having to open a lot of menus. Excel displays the Standard and Formatting toolbar when you first start the program.

To help with some special tasks, such as formatting charts, you can open additional Toolbars or Toolboxes. Toolboxes differ from Toolbars in that you can move them around the screen, placing them wherever they're convenient.

Selecting Commands from a Toolbar or Toolbox

To select a command from a Toolbar or Toolbox, place your mouse pointer over the command's button and click.

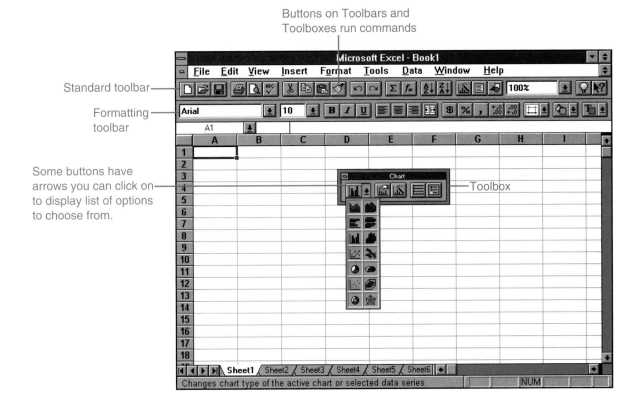

Buttons on Toolbars and Toolboxes run commands

Standard toolbar

Formatting toolbar

Some buttons have arrows you can click on to display list of options to choose from.

Toolbox

USING TOOLBARS AND TOOLBOXES

Opening a Toolbar or Toolbox

1 Click on the View menu or press **Alt+V**.

2 Click on the Toolbars command or press **T**.

3 Select the name of the toolbar you want to open. An X in the box indicates that the Toolbar is currently selected or displayed.

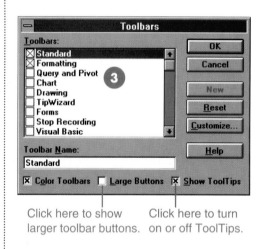

Click here to show larger toolbar buttons.

Click here to turn on or off ToolTips.

4 Click on the **OK** button or press **Enter**.

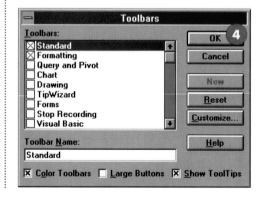

What Does It Do?

If you're not sure what a particular command button does, place your mouse pointer over the command button. Excel displays a ToolTip directly under the button that provides the name of the button.

Tool

Description

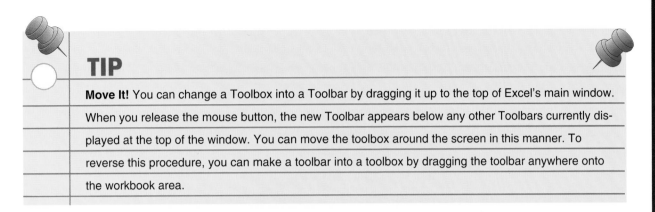

TIP

Move It! You can change a Toolbox into a Toolbar by dragging it up to the top of Excel's main window. When you release the mouse button, the new Toolbar appears below any other Toolbars currently displayed at the top of the window. You can move the toolbox around the screen in this manner. To reverse this procedure, you can make a toolbar into a toolbox by dragging the toolbar anywhere onto the workbook area.

LEARNING THE LINGO

Button: An on-screen button object that you can click to select a specific Excel command.

Toolbar: A stationary row of buttons at the top or bottom of Excel's main window.

Toolbox: A small, movable box containing command buttons.

Beginning Excel Tasks

GETTING HELP

Why Use On-line Help?

Because Excel is a powerful program containing hundreds of commands, Microsoft added a comprehensive on-line help system, so you can find answers to your questions quickly. Access Excel's help system from the **Help** menu or by simply pressing **F1**.

The search button opens a dialog box into which you can type a Help topic you want to find.

The contents button returns you to the contents list.

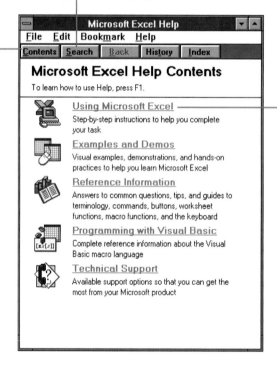

Clicking on a jump term displays an explanation of the term.

Getting Help on a Specific Topic

1 Click on the **Help** menu or press **Alt+H**.

2 Click on the **Contents** command or press **C**.

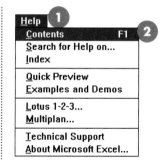

3 Click on the **S**earch button or press **Alt+S**.

4 Type the topic for which you need help, and press **Enter**.

5 Select a topic from the list at the bottom of the dialog box.

6 Select the **G**o To button or press **Alt+G**.

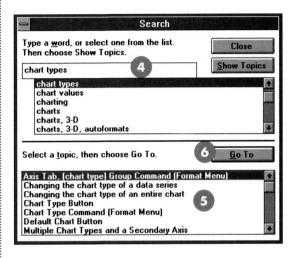

7 Read the **Help** text for the topic, using the scroll bar or the **PgDn** and **PgUp** keys to scroll the text.

8 Click on any jump terms you want to read about.

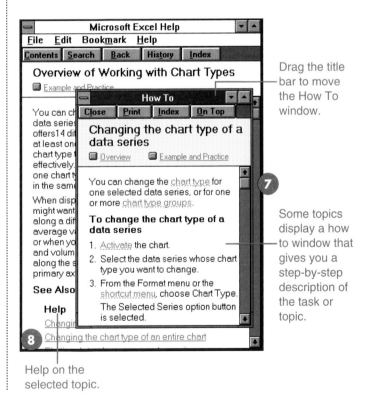

Drag the title bar to move the How To window.

Some topics display a how to window that gives you a step-by-step description of the task or topic.

Help on the selected topic.

Beginning Excel Tasks

GETTING HELP

9 Double-click the **Help window's Control box** to close Help or select the Exit command from the Help File menu.

Help Is On the Way!

Use the tool-bar's handy Help tool to get information about any object on your screen. Just click on the **Help** tool on the Standard tool-bar, and then click on the object with which you need help.

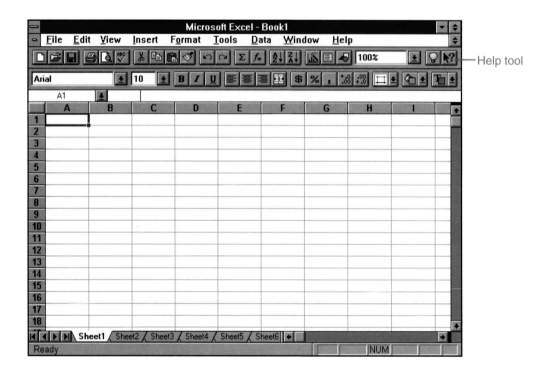

Help tool

OPENING AN EXISTING WORKBOOK

Why Open an Existing Workbook?

When Excel first appears on your screen, it opens a blank workbook window called **Book1**.

If you're starting a new workbook, you can use this default workbook. However, you'll often want to open a workbook that you previously created and saved to your hard disk. To open an existing workbook, select **Open** from the File menu.

Opening an Existing Workbook

1 Click on the File menu or press **Alt+F**.

2 Click on the Open command or press **O**.

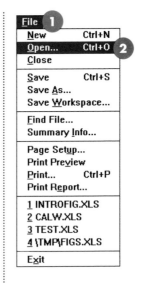

3 If necessary, select a drive from the Drives drop-down list.

4 Double-click the directory that contains the file, or highlight it and press **Enter**.

5 Double-click the file you want to open, or highlight it and select **OK** or press **Enter**.

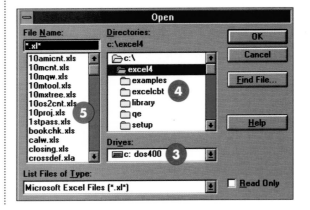

OPENING AN EXISTING WORKBOOK

Exercise

In this exercise, you'll open the file **SALES.XLS**, which you'll find in Excel's **EXAMPLES** directory.

1 Select **O**pen from the **F**ile menu, or press **Ctrl+O**.

2 Select the **EXAMPLES** directory, and then press **Enter**, or double-click on the **EXAMPLES** directory.

3 Select **SALES.XLS**, and then select **OK**, or press **Enter**.

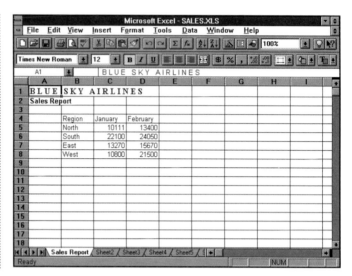

QUICK REFRESHER

To use a list box from the keyboard, press **Tab** until the blinking text cursor appears in the text box or until the currently selected item in the text box is highlighted. (When the item in the text box contains wild card characters, such as asterisks, as it does in the File Name text box, you must press **Tab** once more to make a dotted box appear in the list box.) Then use the **up** or **down** arrow keys to highlight the item in the list.

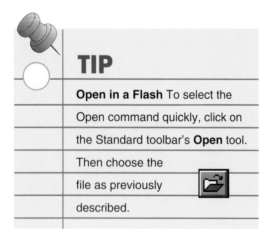

TIP

Open in a Flash To select the Open command quickly, click on the Standard toolbar's **Open** tool. Then choose the file as previously described.

LEARNING THE LINGO

File: Your workbooks are stored on your hard disk in a *file*, a collection of related data stored as a single unit.

Directory: Directories are like little file cabinets on your hard drive that help you organize your files. They can contain either files or other directories.

OPENING A NEW WORKBOOK

Why Open a New Workbook?

If you've already used Book1 and want to start yet another workbook, you can do it by selecting **New** from the **File** menu.

When you open a new workbook, Excel names it something like Book2. Before doing any work on the new workbook, you should save it under a new name. See the "Saving a Workbook" task.

Opening a New Workbook

1 Click on the **File** menu or press **Alt+F**.

2 Click on the **New Command** or press **N**.

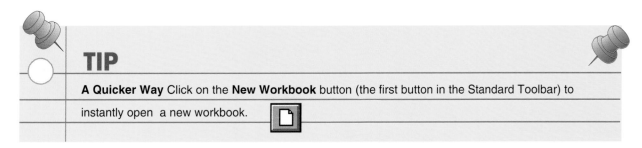

TIP

A Quicker Way Click on the **New Workbook** button (the first button in the Standard Toolbar) to instantly open a new workbook.

CLOSING A WORKBOOK

Why Close a Workbook?

After you're finished viewing a workbook, you may want to close it, which removes the workbook from your screen and from your computer's memory. (The workbook still exists on your disk, however, so you can open it again any time you like.) By closing workbooks you no longer currently need, you'll have fewer Excel windows to manage. You'll also give Excel more memory with which to work.

Closing a Workbook

1 Click on the File menu or press **Alt+F**.

2 Click on the Close command or press **C**.

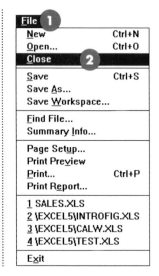

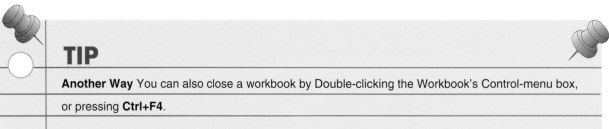

TIP

Another Way You can also close a workbook by Double-clicking the Workbook's Control-menu box, or pressing **Ctrl+F4**.

What If It Asks to Save?

If you make changes to a workbook and then try to close it, Excel asks if you want to save your changes. Select Yes to save the changes, select No to close the workbook without saving the changes, or select Cancel to cancel the Close command.

SAVING A WORKBOOK

Why Save a Workbook?

When you exit Excel, all the workbooks currently open are removed from memory. If you haven't saved any changes, there's no way to get them back. You must save your workbooks to disk so that they will be available to view or edit later. Select **Save** from the **File** menu to save your workbooks.

Saving a Workbook

1 Click on the **File** menu or press **Alt+F**.

2 Click on the **Save** command or press **S**.

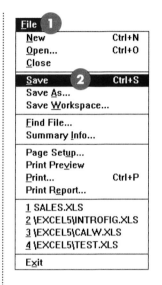

3 Type in the name of the workbook file you want to save it under in the File **Name** text box.

4 If necessary, change to the drive and/or directory in which you wish to save the workbook file.

5 Click on the **OK** button or press **Enter**.

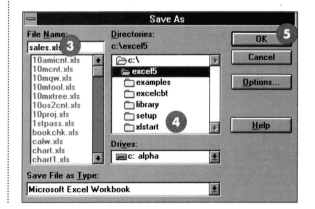

When you type the file name, you don't need to add the extension (which is .XLS for a workbook). Excel adds the appropriate extension automatically.

Beginning Excel Tasks

SAVING A WORKBOOK

Saving a Workbook with a Different Name

Often, you need to save a workbook under a new name. You might want to do this so you can have two copies of the same sheet (one for experimentation) or because you started a new workbook and need to give it a name other than the default name Excel assigned to it (that is, Book1). To save a workbook under a new name, select Save **As** from the **F**ile menu and type a new name in the File Name text box and then press **Enter**.

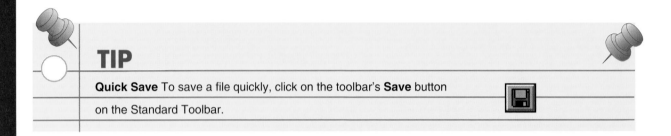
LEARNING THE LINGO

File extension: Most file names end with a period followed by one to three characters. These characters, called the file name's extension, identify the file's type. For example, all Excel workbooks have the .XLS extension, whereas Excel charts have an .XLC extension and templates have an .XLT extension.

SEARCHING FOR A WORKBOOK

Why Search for a Workbook?

There may be times when you can't remember where you saved a workbook or
what you named it. Luckily, Excel offers a finding feature. You can search for your
workbook files by selecting the Find File command button from the Open dialog
box and select **Search**.

You can save the
search criteria.

Indicate what file
to search.

Indicate what drive
and/or directory to
search in.

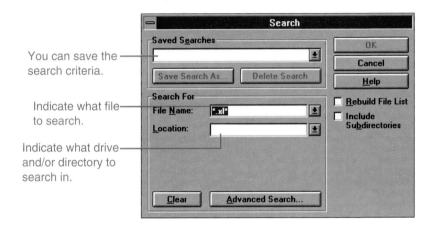

Finding Files

1. Click on the File menu or press **Alt+F**.

2. Click on the Open command or press **O**.

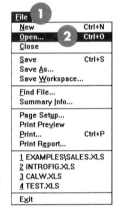

3. Click on the Find File button or press **Alt+F**.

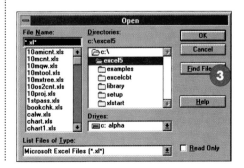

SEARCHING FOR A WORKBOOK

4 Type the workbook file you want to find in the File **Name** text box.

5 Type the drive and/or directory to search in the **Location** text box. You can also select the drop-down list arrow and select a location from the list. Select **Include Subdirectories** check box if necessary.

6 Click on the **OK** button or press **Enter**.

7 Select a workbook file from the Listed Files list.

8 If you want to Open the workbook file, click on the **Open** button or press **Alt+O**.

9 If you want to exit the File Find dialog box without opening a workbook file, select the **Close** button or press **Enter**.

10 If you want to search again, click on the **Search** button or press **Alt+S**.

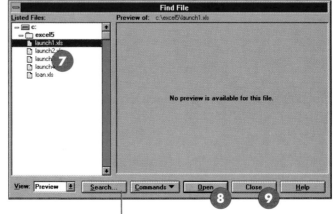

Click here to search for another file.

Why Quit Excel?

When you're finished working with Excel, you'll want to quit the application, which closes Excel's main window and removes the program from your computer's memory. You should always end your Excel sessions this way. Never end your session by turning off your computer, as you could lose unsaved work and possibly even damage data on your hard disk.

Quitting Excel

1 Click on the **File** menu or press **Alt+F**.

2 Click on the **Exit** command or press **X**.

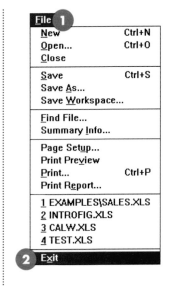

3 If prompted, select **Yes** to save the changes or **No** to quit Excel without saving the changes.

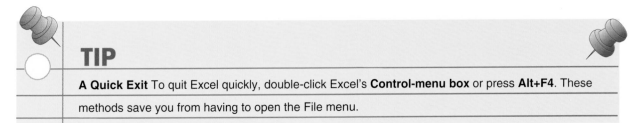

TIP

A Quick Exit To quit Excel quickly, double-click Excel's **Control-menu box** or press **Alt+F4**. These methods save you from having to open the File menu.

Beginning Excel Tasks

PART 2

Building a Worksheet

This part describes Excel tasks that you need to know to build and manipulate worksheets and workbooks. When you have finished this part, you will be able to enter data of various types into the worksheet, create mathematical functions, and edit cells.

- Selecting Cells
- Entering Labels
- Entering Values
- Entering Dates and Times
- Entering Formulas
- Using Cell Ranges in Formulas
- Using Excel's Built-In Functions

SELECTING CELLS

Why Select Cells?

Most operations that you can perform on a single cell you can also perform on groups of cells. Simply select the group of cells before issuing the command. You can select rows, columns, rectangular blocks, contiguous cells, 3-D cells, or entire worksheets.

The block of cells D4:G6 is highlighted to create a range.

The white box is the cell cursor.

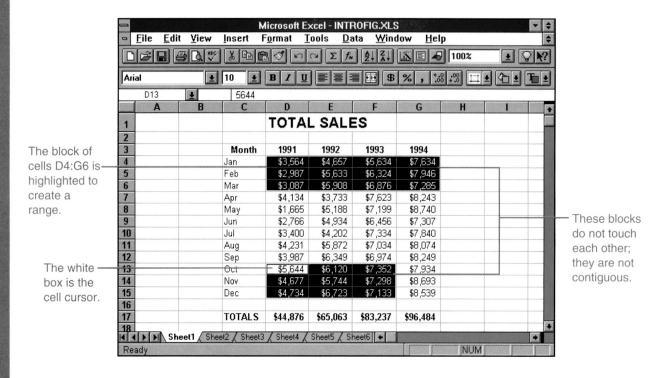

These blocks do not touch each other; they are not contiguous.

To select all of the worksheets in a workbook, click the right mouse button on any sheet tab to display the sheet tab shortcut menu and then select the Select All Sheets command.

LEARNING THE LINGO

Contiguous: Selected cells or ranges that are adjacent to one another.

Range: A group of rectangular blocks of cells.

QUICK REFRESHER

To *drag* the mouse pointer, hold down the left mouse button while you move the mouse, dragging the pointer across the screen.

Selecting Groups of Cells

To select a block of cells, drag the mouse pointer across the cells. Or move to the first cell in the range, hold down the Shift key, and use the arrow keys to expand the block.

Click on the column heading to select an entire column.

	A	B	C	D	E	F	G	H	I	
1										
2			Month	1991	1992	1993	1994			
3			Jan	$3,564	$4,657	$5,634	$7,634			
4			FEb	$2,987	$5,633	$6,324	$7,946			
5			Mar	$3,087	$5,908	$6,876	$7,285			
6			Apr	$4,134	$3,733	$7,623	$8,243			
7			May	$1,665	$5,188	$7,199	$8,740			
8			Jun	$2,766	$4,934	$6,456	$7,307			
9			Jul	$3,400	$4,202	$7,334	$7,840			
10			Aug	$4,231	$5,872	$7,034	$8,074			
11			Sep	$3,987	$6,349	$6,974	$8,249			
12			Oct	$5,644	$6,120	$7,352	$7,934			
13			Nov	$4,677	$5,744	$7,298	$8,693			
14			Dec	$4,734	$6,723	$7,133	$8,539			
15										
16			TOTALS	$44,876	$65,063	$83,237	$96,484			
17										
18										

Sheet1 / Sheet2 / Sheet3 / Sheet4 / Sheet5 / Sheet6

Ready   NUM

Click on a row heading to select an entire row. Click here to select the entire worksheet.

Hold the Shift key and click on the sheet tabs to select the same ranges in other sheets.

To select nonadjacent cells or ranges, hold down the CTRL key as you select a range.

Exercise

Practice the cell-selection techniques by selecting a block of cells ranging from B2 to F10.

1 Click on cell **B2**, or use the arrow keys to position the cell cursor there.

2 Hold down the left mouse button, and move the mouse pointer to cell F10, then release the mouse button. Or hold down **Shift**, and use the arrow keys to position the cell cursor at **F10.**

Start the block here by clicking or positioning the cell cursor with the arrow keys.

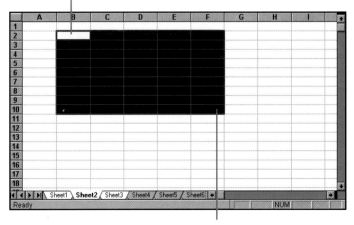

Drag the mouse pointer to cell F10, or hold down Shift and press the right and down arrow keys until F10 is highlighted.

Building a Worksheet

ENTERING LABELS

What Is a Label?

The cells that make up a worksheet can hold several types of data, including labels, values, and formulas. Labels are entries that cannot be calculated, such as text in row and column headings and explanatory notes. You'll learn about values and formulas later in this book.

Column headings are labels.

The title is a label.

Row headings are labels.

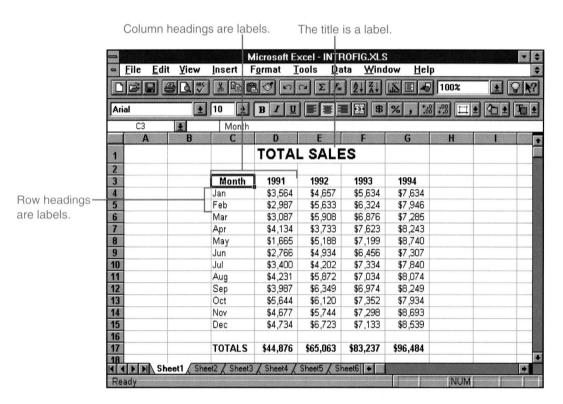

LEARNING THE LINGO

Label: A series of characters that have no numerical value. A label is usually used for headings and notations.

Entering a Label into a Cell

1 Move the cell cursor to the cell you want.

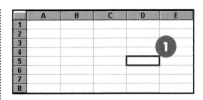

2 Type the label, and then press **Enter**.

Text appears in the formula bar as you type.

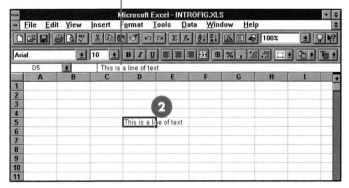

The *formula bar* always displays the contents of the current cell. In the case of text, the cell and the formula bar show the same thing. However, when the current cell contains a formula, the formula bar displays the formula, and the cell displays the value calculated by the formula. You'll learn more about formulas later in the book.

QUICK REFRESHER

To move the cell cursor to a cell, click on it or use the arrow keys to position the cell cursor. You can also press **F5** and enter the specific cell to which you want to go, or use the worksheet movement keys such as **PgDn** and **Ctrl+←**.

Building a Worksheet

ENTERING LABELS

Changing a Value to a Label

When you enter a number into a cell, Excel assumes the number is a value rather than a label. This assumption creates problems when you need to enter a number like a zip code or phone number, which should be treated as text. Luckily, there's an easy way to tell Excel when a number is a text value. Simply begin the text entry with a single quote ('), which is the symbol to the left of your Enter key.

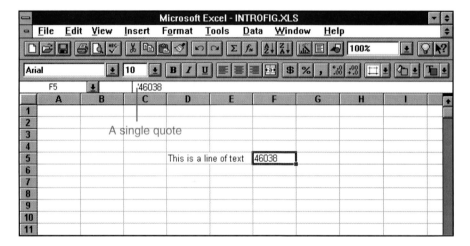

TIP

Look and See As you'll learn later, by default, values are right-aligned in cells and labels are left-aligned. This is an easy way to quickly determine whether an entry is a value or a label.

ENTERING VALUES

What Is a Value?

A *value*, simply stated, is a number upon which you can perform a calculation. (Numbers such as ZIP codes and phone numbers are considered labels rather than values because they're not used in calculations.)

Manipulating values is the whole reason for setting up a worksheet in the first place. No matter what type of worksheet you create, sooner or later you're going to need to enter values into cells. Other cells in your worksheet then use these values in formulas to calculate the results you need. You'll learn how to enter formulas later in the book.

Formula in D17

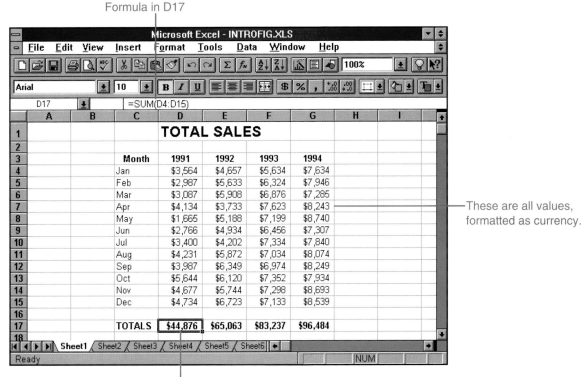

These are all values, formatted as currency.

This value is the result of a formula, as you can see by looking at the formula bar.

Building a Worksheet

ENTERING VALUES

Entering a Value into a Cell

1 Move the cell cursor to the cell.

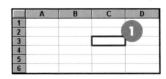

2 Type the value, and press **Enter**.

The value appears in the formula bar as you type.

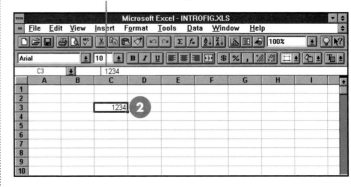

Exercise

To see the difference between a regular number and a text number, type the number **08764** with and without a single quote.

1 Move to the cell.

2 Type 08764, and press **Enter**.

3 Move to a different cell.

4 Type '**08764** (starting with a single quote), and press **Enter**.

Excel removes the leading zero for values.

A number without a single quote is treated as a value.

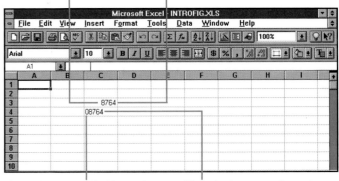

A number preceded by a single quote is treated as a label.

The single quote character does not appear in the cell.

ENTERING DATES AND TIMES

How Does Excel Handle Dates and Times?

Excel treats dates and times as values, so that you can perform calculations on them. To make the dates more readable than plain values, however, Excel offers some special formatting features. When you enter a date or time, Excel attempts to match it with one of its standard formats, adding capital letters and punctuation where necessary.

You can enter and display dates in any of these formats.

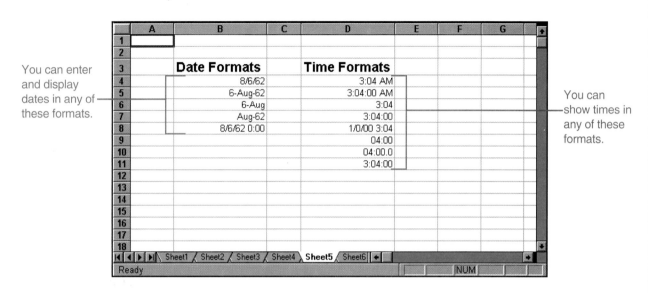

You can show times in any of these formats.

The Way Excel Sees It

Excel stores each date and time in a plain numerical format representing its relationship to January 1, 1900. For example, January 1, 1901, 5:30 PM, would be 367.729. However, Excel realizes that you would rather see dates and times in a more readable format, so it formats them for screen display as you are accustomed to seeing them.

TIP

Determining the Format You don't have to type a date or time exactly in the format expected by Excel. Excel will determine the format that most closely matches what you've typed and change your entry accordingly. For example, if you enter **May 14**, Excel automatically displays the date as **14-May**.

45

ENTERING DATES AND TIMES

Entering a Date or Time

1 Move to the cell where you want to enter a date or time.

2 Type the date or time, and press **Enter**.

The date or time appears in the formula bar as you type.

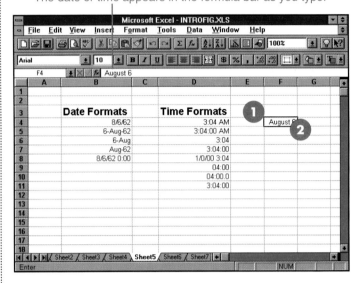

3 If you are not happy with the format of the date or time, click the right mouse button and select the Format Cells command from the shortcut menu that appears. You can also select the Cells command from the Format menu.

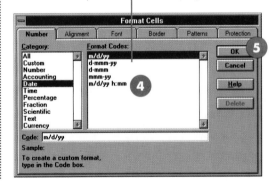

4 Select the date or time format of your choice.

5 Click on the OK button or press Enter.

Select the format in which you want the date displayed.

ENTERING FORMULAS

What Is a Formula?

A *formula* is an instruction to perform some math calculation on the values in one or more cells. The formulas you enter into your worksheet may be as simple as the sum of two cells or as complex as determining the standard deviation of a table of values.

Formulas can include various elements, including values, cell references, sheet references, operators, or worksheet functions. These elements are calculated based on rules of *operator precedence*, which dictate in what order various math operations are performed. You can change the order of operations by adding parentheses to a formula so that whatever is within the parentheses is calculated first.

Order	Symbol	Meaning
1	^	exponentiation
2	* /	multiplication and division
3	+ -	addition and subtraction

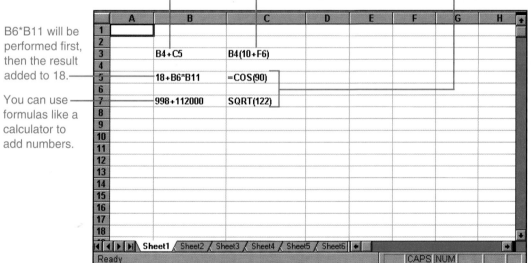

A simple formula adding the contents of two cells.

10+F6 will be performed first because of the parentheses.

Built-in functions make complicated math operations simple.

B6*B11 will be performed first, then the result added to 18.

You can use formulas like a calculator to add numbers.

ENTERING FORMULAS

Entering a Formula

1 Move to the cell.

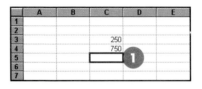

2 Type an equals sign (=), and then the formula.

The formula appears in the formula bar as you type.

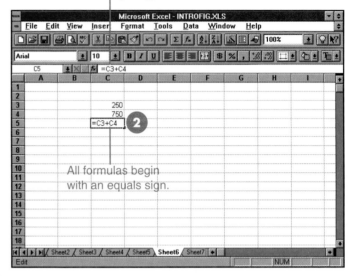

All formulas begin with an equals sign.

3 Press **Enter** to display the formula result in the cell.

The formula still appears in the formula bar.

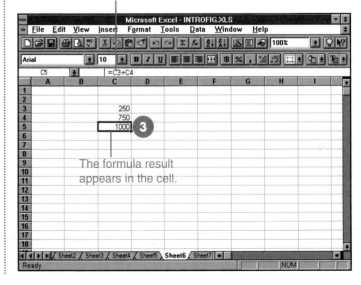

The formula result appears in the cell.

Exercise

In this exercise, you'll average the values in three cells using Excel's math operators.

1 Enter **234** in cell D3.

2 Enter **365** in cell D4.

3 Enter **419** in cell D5.

4 Enter **Average:** in cell C7.

5 Move to cell D7.

6 Type the formula **=(D3+D4+D5)/3** and press **Enter**.

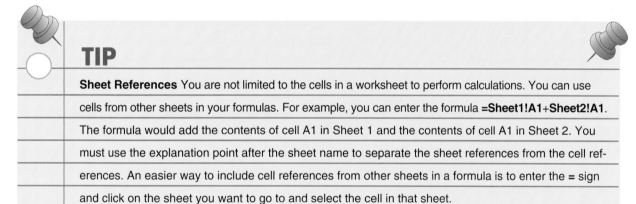

TIP

Sheet References You are not limited to the cells in a worksheet to perform calculations. You can use cells from other sheets in your formulas. For example, you can enter the formula **=Sheet1!A1+Sheet2!A1**. The formula would add the contents of cell A1 in Sheet 1 and the contents of cell A1 in Sheet 2. You must use the explanation point after the sheet name to separate the sheet references from the cell references. An easier way to include cell references from other sheets in a formula is to enter the = sign and click on the sheet you want to go to and select the cell in that sheet.

LEARNING THE LINGO

Cell reference: You create a cell reference by typing the cell's column letter followed by the cell's row number (that is, **B12**).

Operators: Excel supports many operators that you can use in your formulas, including addition (+), subtraction (-), multiplication (*), division (/), and percentage (%).

Worksheet functions: These are built-in functions that you can use to calculate values. Some functions are SUM, which calculates sums; AVERAGE, which calculates averages; and SQRT, which calculates square roots. There are hundreds of worksheet functions, all of which are listed in the *Worksheet Function Reference* that came with your copy of Excel.

Operator precedence: The order in which arithmetic operations are performed, also called "order of operations."

Building a Worksheet

USING CELL RANGES IN FORMULAS

Why Use Ranges?

Often, you need to refer to all the cells in a block. Using two simple cell references separated by a colon (called a *cell range*), you can refer to any block of cells you like, even an entire worksheet.

Specifying Ranges

1 When you are ready to enter a cell range in a formula, click on the first cell in the range or type the cell name.

First cell address in the formula.

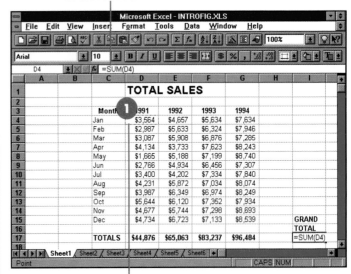

First cell in the range.

2 Type a colon (:).

3 Click on the last cell in the range or type the cell name.

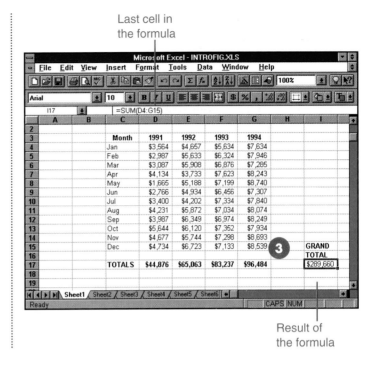

Last cell in
the formula

Result of
the formula

LEARNING THE LINGO

Cell range: A cell range refers to a block of cells and consists of two cell references separated by a colon.

Building a Worksheet

USING EXCEL'S BUILT-IN FUNCTIONS

What Are Functions?

If you look in the *Worksheet Function Reference* that came with your copy of Excel, you'll see that Excel provides hundreds of functions you can use to simplify calculations in your worksheets. For example, while you can sum a series of cells by typing a formula like **=A1+A2+A3+A4+A5**, it's much easier to use Excel's SUM function: **=SUM(A1:A5)**.

Functions are made up of a function name followed by the function's arguments enclosed in parentheses. Multiple arguments are separated by commas. Function arguments can be just about any type of data, depending on the function. You'll mostly use numbers, cell references, formulas, and possibly text as arguments.

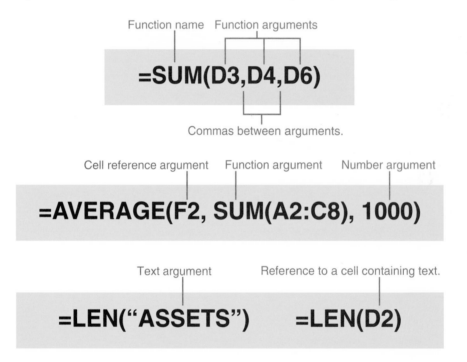

Function name   Function arguments

=SUM(D3,D4,D6)

Commas between arguments.

Cell reference argument   Function argument   Number argument

=AVERAGE(F2, SUM(A2:C8), 1000)

Text argument   Reference to a cell containing text.

=LEN("ASSETS")   =LEN(D2)

QUICK REFRESHER

Remember, if a function appears at the beginning of a formula, it must start with an equals (=) sign.

Inserting a Function into a Worksheet

1 Move to the cell into which you want to enter the function.

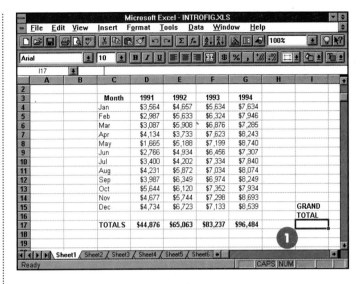

2 Select the **Insert** menu or press **Alt+I**.

3 Select the **Function** command or press **F**.

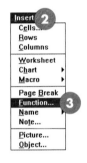

4 Select a category from the Function **Category** list box.

5 Select a function from the Function **Name** list box.

6 Select the **Next** button.

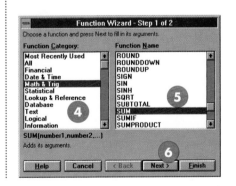

Building a Worksheet

USING EXCEL'S BUILT-IN FUNCTIONS

7 Finish the formula by typing the arguments needed by the function you selected. The argument requirements are different depending on the function you selected.

8 Click on the **Finish** button or press **Alt+F**.

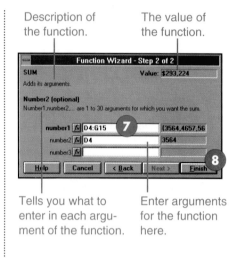

Description of the function.

The value of the function.

Tells you what to enter in each argument of the function.

Enter arguments for the function here.

Once you've learned a few functions, you can type them directly into a cell, rather than selecting them from the Paste Function dialog box. Often it's faster to type them yourself. How-ever, the Function Wizard helps you sort through the hundreds of functions supported by Excel.

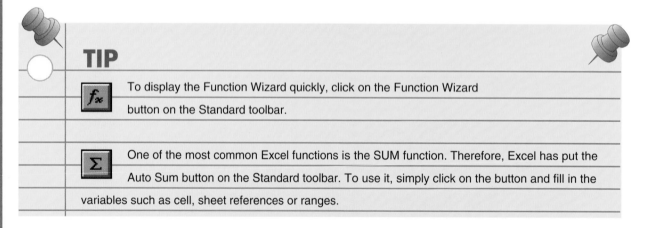

TIP

To display the Function Wizard quickly, click on the Function Wizard button on the Standard toolbar.

One of the most common Excel functions is the SUM function. Therefore, Excel has put the Auto Sum button on the Standard toolbar. To use it, simply click on the button and fill in the variables such as cell, sheet references or ranges.

LEARNING THE LINGO

Arguments: The values functions need in order to calculate a result. A function's arguments are enclosed in parentheses.

PART 3

Editing and Formatting a Worksheet

This part describes how to change your worksheet's contents and format. When you have finished this part, you will be able to copy, move, insert, delete, find, and sort cells; change cell formats; adjust the alignment of cell data; modify cell widths and heights; and add borders and shading to areas of your worksheet.

- Editing Cell Contents
- Moving and Copying Cells
- Inserting Rows and Columns
- Deleting Rows and Columns
- Clearing Cells
- Finding Data in Cells
- Replacing Data in Cells
- Sorting Data
- Changing Number Formats
- Aligning Data in Cells
- Changing Cell Widths
- Changing Fonts and Text Attributes

EDITING CELL CONTENTS

Why Edit Cell Contents?

Worksheets can grow to contain dozens, even hundreds, of values and formulas. Sooner or later, you'll discover an error in a cell or need to update a formula to reflect changes in the worksheet. Luckily, editing the contents of a cell is as easy as editing a document with a word processor. You only need to select the cell to edit and then change the contents of the cell in the formula bar.

Editing Cell Contents

1 Move to the cell whose contents you want to edit.

The contents of the selected cell appear in the formula bar.

	A	B	C	D	E	F	G	H	I
2									
3			Month	1991	1992	1993	1994		
4			Jan	$3,564	$4,657	$5,634	$7,634		
5			Feb	$2,987	$5,633	$6,324	$7,946		
6			Mar	$3,087	$5,908	$6,876	$7,285		
7			Apr	$4,134	$3,733	$7,623	$8,243		
8			May	$1,665	$5,188	$7,199	$8,740		
9			Jun	$2,766	$4,934	$6,456	$7,307		
10			Jul	$3,400	$4,202	$7,334	$7,840		
11			Aug	$4,231	$5,872	$7,034	$8,074		
12			Sep	$3,987	$6,349	$6,974	$8,249		
13			Oct	$5,644	$6,120	$7,352	$7,934		
14			Nov	$4,677	$5,744	$7,298	$8,693		
15			Dec	$4,734	$6,723	$7,133	$8,539		
16									
17			TOTALS	$44,876	$65,063	$83,237	$96,484		
18									
19									

G17 =SUM(G4:G15)

2 Double-click on the cell or press **F2**.

LEARNING THE LINGO

Insertion cursor: A blinking vertical bar that shows where the next typed character will appear.

Status Bar: An area at the bottom of Excel's main window that displays messages about the worksheet's status.

3 Edit the data or formula as desired.

Edit indicator in the Status Bar

4 When finished editing, press **Enter.**

ENTER 4

With earlier versions of Excel, you had to edit your text in the formula bar rather than directly in the cell. If you prefer to edit in this manner, click on the cell you want to edit and then click anywhere in the Formula Bar and begin editing. You also have some editing buttons available to you in the Formula Bar. Click on the X button to cancel your edit and the check mark button to accept your edit.

TIP

It Won't Work If you can't seem to edit your data when you double-click on a cell, the editing in cell feature may be turned off. To turn it back on, select the **O**ptions command from the **T**ools menu and click on the Edit tab. Select the **E**dit Directly in Cell check box and click on OK.

Replacing If you do not want to edit the contents of a cell but rather replace the entire thing, simply typeover the text and press the **Enter** key.

Editing and Formatting a Worksheet

MOVING AND COPYING CELLS

Why Move or Copy Cells?

As you manipulate a worksheet, you may need to copy or move blocks of data to different locations. For example, you might want to do this to reorganize the way a worksheet is laid out, or you might want to start a table that contains similar data to an existing table.

When you move or copy formulas that contain cell references, you don't have to worry about changing the cell references in your formula; the formula changes to take its new location into account. For example, if you have **=B2+B3** in cell B4, and move the formula to cell D4, the formula becomes **=D2+D3**.

Moving or Copying Cells

1 Move to the upper left cell in the block you want to move.

2 Holding down the left mouse button, drag the mouse pointer to the lower right cell of the block.

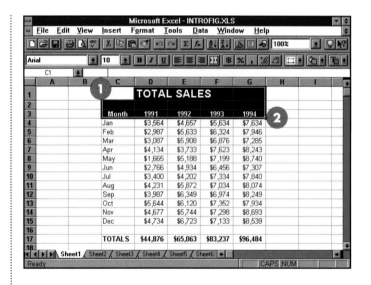

3 (Optional) If you are copying (rather than moving), hold down **Ctrl** while you perform the next step.

58

4 Move the mouse cursor to the edge of the highlighted block, and hold down the left mouse button while you drag the block to its new location.

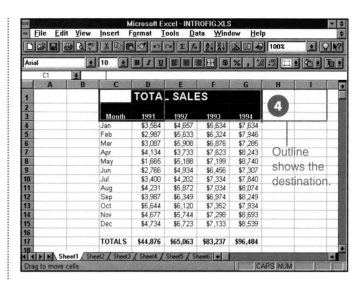

TIP

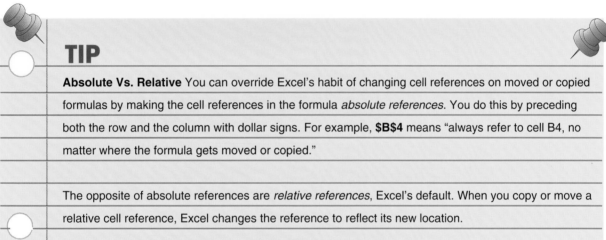

Absolute Vs. Relative You can override Excel's habit of changing cell references on moved or copied formulas by making the cell references in the formula *absolute references*. You do this by preceding both the row and the column with dollar signs. For example, **$B$4** means "always refer to cell B4, no matter where the formula gets moved or copied."

The opposite of absolute references are *relative references*, Excel's default. When you copy or move a relative cell reference, Excel changes the reference to reflect its new location.

Editing and Formatting a Worksheet

MOVING AND COPYING CELLS

If you're unable to drag a block of cells with your mouse, you need to select the Cell Drag and Drop option. To do this, select the Options command from the Tools menu, select the Edit tab, and then select the Allow Cell Drag And Drop check box.

Select this option to allow the dragging of blocks with the mouse.

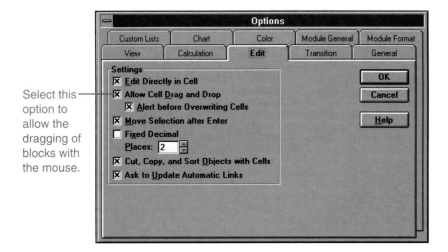

Moving and Copying to Other Sheets

You are not limited to only copying and moving your data within a worksheet. You can copy and move your data to other worksheets in the workbook or other workbooks for that matter. Select the block of text you want to copy or move and click on the **Cut** (select this button if you want to move data) or **Copy** buttons on the Standard toolbar. Move to the sheet or workbook you want to move or copy the data to and select the **Paste** button on the button bar. The data will be moved or copied.

cut   copy   paste

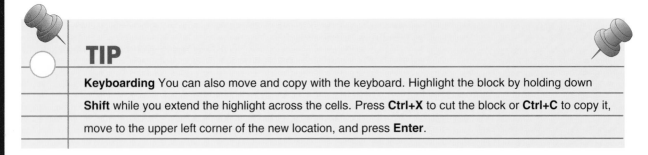

TIP

Keyboarding You can also move and copy with the keyboard. Highlight the block by holding down **Shift** while you extend the highlight across the cells. Press **Ctrl+X** to cut the block or **Ctrl+C** to copy it, move to the upper left corner of the new location, and press **Enter**.

Exercise

Create the simple worksheet shown in this figure. Then move the block of data from **B2:D4** to **C20:E22**.

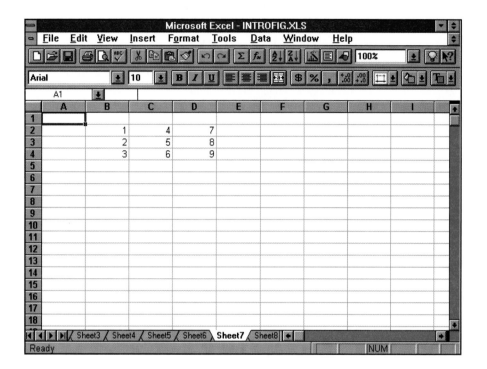

Using the mouse:

1   Move to cell **B2**.

2   Holding down the left mouse button, drag the mouse pointer to **D4**, and then release the mouse button.

3   Move the mouse pointer to one of the block's edges.

4   Hold down the left mouse button and drag the block to position its upper left corner at **C20**. Then release the mouse button.

Editing and Formatting a Worksheet

INSERTING ROWS AND COLUMNS

Why Insert Rows and Columns?

The more complicated a worksheet becomes, the more likely it is that you will need to make changes, like adding new data. You can easily add entire rows or columns of cells by using Excel's Insert command. When you add cells, Excel automatically adjusts moved cell references to reflect their new location.

Before you insert a row or column, you must indicate where you want it. Do this by selecting an existing row or column that's to the right or below the location of where you want the new one to be. Use this table as a guideline:

To select	Use the mouse	Or the keyboard
A row	Click on the row number	Press **Shift+Spacebar** while cell cursor is in the row.
A column	Click the column letter	Press **Ctrl+Spacebar** while cell cursor is in the column.

Inserting a Row or Column

1 Select the row or column below or to the right of where you want the new row or column to be (see the table above).

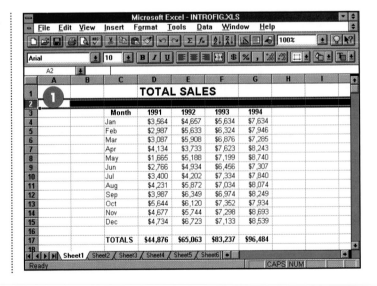

2 Click on the Insert menu or press **Alt+I**.

3 Click on either the **Rows** or **Columns** command or press **R** or **C**.

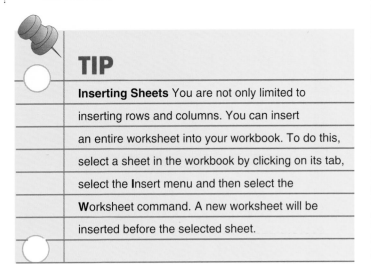

TIP

Quick Insert To quickly insert a row or column, click the right mouse button to display the shortcut menu and then select the Insert command.

TIP

Inserting Sheets You are not only limited to inserting rows and columns. You can insert an entire worksheet into your workbook. To do this, select a sheet in the workbook by clicking on its tab, select the Insert menu and then select the Worksheet command. A new worksheet will be inserted before the selected sheet.

Editing and Formatting a Worksheet

DELETING ROWS AND COLUMNS

Why Delete Rows and Columns?

If you find that a column you've created in your worksheet is not needed, you can simply delete it. All remaining columns shift, and cell references are automatically adjusted.

You must select the row or column to delete before you can remove it. Use this table as a guideline:

To select	Use the mouse	Or the keyboard
A row	Click on the row number	Press **Shift+Spacebar** while cell cursor is in the row.
A column	Click the column letter	Press **Ctrl+Spacebar** while cell cursor is in the column.

Deleting a Row or Column

1 Select the row or column you want to delete (see the table above).

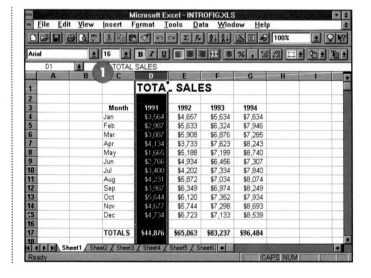

2 Click the **Edit** menu or press **Alt+E**.

3 Click on the **Delete** command or press **D**.

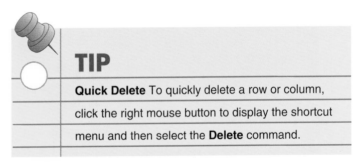

You are not only limited to deleting rows and columns in a worksheet. You can delete an entire worksheet from your workbook. To do this, select a sheet in the workbook by clicking on its tab, select the Edit menu and then select the Delete Sheet command. The worksheet will be deleted from the workbook after you select OK when you are asked if you are sure you want to delete the worksheet in the next box.

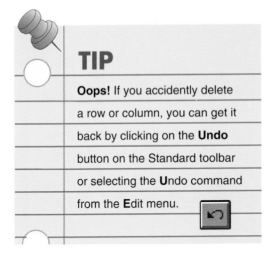

TIP

Oops! If you accidently delete a row or column, you can get it back by clicking on the **Undo** button on the Standard toolbar or selecting the **U**ndo command from the **E**dit menu.

TIP

Quick Delete To quickly delete a row or column, click the right mouse button to display the shortcut menu and then select the **Delete** command.

CLEARING CELLS

Why Clear Cells?

Once you enter data into a cell, you're not stuck with it forever. Excel allows you to clear data, formats, or notes from any cell at any time.

There's a difference between clearing and deleting. When you delete a cell, you remove both the cell and its contents from your worksheet. When you clear a cell, only the cell's contents are deleted. The cell itself remains in place. Don't let it fool you that you press the Delete key to clear—not delete—a cell.

Clearing a Cell

1 Move to the cell you want to clear.

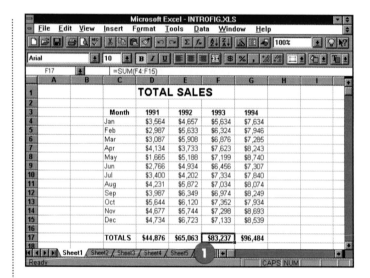

2 Click on the **E**dit menu or press **Alt+E**.

3 Click on the **Clear** command or press **A**.

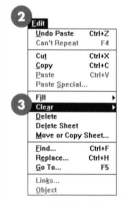

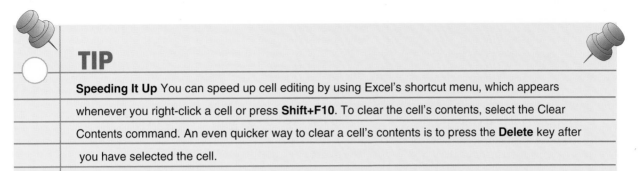

TIP

Speeding It Up You can speed up cell editing by using Excel's shortcut menu, which appears whenever you right-click a cell or press **Shift+F10**. To clear the cell's contents, select the Clear Contents command. An even quicker way to clear a cell's contents is to press the **Delete** key after you have selected the cell.

LEARNING THE LINGO

Cell format: A cell's format is the way a cell displays its data, including the number type, the alignment of data within the cell, and text styles, such as bold or italics.

Editing and Formatting a Worksheet

FINDING DATA IN CELLS

Why Find Data in Cells?

While it's easy enough to edit a cell's contents on the formula bar, you may at times find that you can't locate the cell you want. For example, you may be looking for the cell that contains the grand total of the payroll account. Luckily, Excel provides an easy way to find cells.

Finding Cells Containing Specific Data

1 Click on the **Edit** menu or press **Alt+E**.

2 Click on the **Find** command or press **F**.

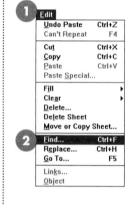

3 Type the data you want to find in the **Fi**nd What text box.

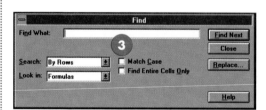

Click on the **Find Next** button or press **Enter**.

 To find the next occurrence of the data, select the **Find Next** button again.

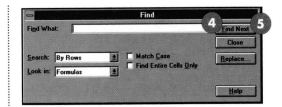

TIP

Replacing Data If you want to find a cell so you can replace something in it, select the **R**eplace button in the Find dialog box and then see "Replacing Data in Cells," the next task in the book.

TIP

Limiting the Search To limit your search to a specific block of cells, highlight the cells before you select the **F**ind command. Excel then searches only the cells in the block.

Editing and Formatting a Worksheet

REPLACING DATA IN CELLS

Why Replace Data?

Replacing is handy when there are many cells you want to edit simultaneously. For example, you might want to change all occurrences of the word **Profit** to **Net Profit**. Excel provides powerful search and replace commands that make this type of editing a snap to perform.

Finding and Replacing Data

1 Click on the **E**dit menu or press **Alt+E**.

2 Click on the **R**eplace command or press **E**.

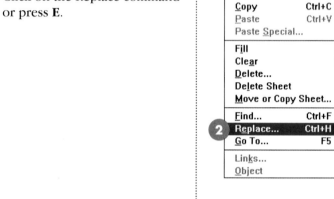

3 Type the data you want to find in the Fi**n**d What text box.

4 Press **Tab**, and type the replacement data in the **R**eplace with text box.

5 To replace all occurrences of the data, select the Replace **A**ll button. Or to replace only the text in the current cell, select the **R**eplace button.

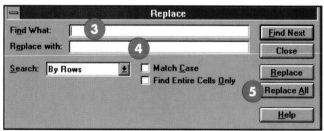

6 If you chose the **R**eplace button, continue selecting it until all the cells containing the text you want to change have been changed.

7 Select the **Close** button. (You don't need to do this if you selected Replace **A**ll.)

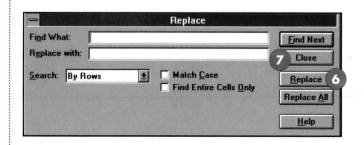

SORTING DATA

Why Sort Data?

Many of your worksheets will contain long lists of data. Often, you'll want to view the data in these lists in a different order. To help you do this, Excel provides a sorting function that can arrange data into alphabetical or numerical order. All you need to do is highlight the data to be sorted and select Excel's Sort command.

Sorting Rows of Data

1 Move to the upper left cell of the block of data to sort.

2 Holding down the left mouse button, drag the mouse pointer to the lower right corner of the block you want to sort.

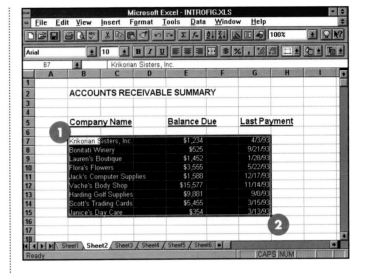

3 Click on the **Data** menu or press **Alt+D**.

4 Click on the **Sort** command or press **S**.

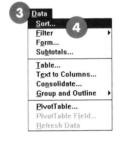

5 If the column you want to sort is not the column displayed in the Sort By text box, click on the arrow to reveal a drop down list and select a column.

SORTING DATA

6 Select the option button next to **Ascending** or **Descending** to determine the order of the sort.

7 Select **OK** or press **Enter**.

TIP

Keep it Together When you select a block of data to sort, make sure you include all of the related data. For example, suppose you have a worksheet containing company names and addresses. If you select only the names, when you sort the rows the names will no longer appear next to their correct addresses.

CHANGING NUMBER FORMATS

Why Change Number Formats?

When you type a number into a cell, Excel displays the number in the general format. But what if you want to display the value as currency? Or suppose you want a number with commas and decimal points? To format a number, you must set the cell's format type. You can do this just by typing your number in the format desired. For example, if you type $23.95, Excel knows that you want the cell formatted as currency. If you need to change the format of a cell, though, select Cells from the Format menu.

Changing Number Formats

1. Move to the cell for which you want to change the number format.

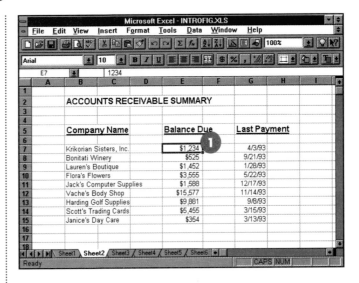

2. Click on the Format menu or press **Alt+O**.

3. Click on the Cells command or press **E**.

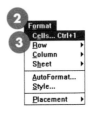

4. Select the format category you want from the **Category** list.

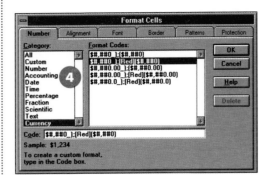

73

CHANGING NUMBER FORMATS

5 Select the format you want from the Format Codes list.

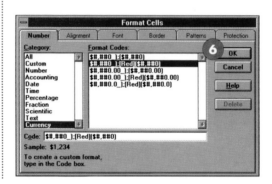

6 Select **OK**, or press **Enter**.

Quick Number Formatting

An easy way to change the number format of values is to use the number formatting buttons on the Formatting toolbar.

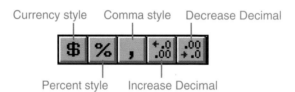

Currency style   Comma style   Decrease Decimal

Percent style   Increase Decimal

ALIGNING DATA IN CELLS

Why Align Data?

Besides adding format codes to your worksheet's cells, you can also add alignment information, which determines where within a cell data is displayed. You can dramatically improve the look of your worksheet with some simple alignment adjustments. Here are some examples:

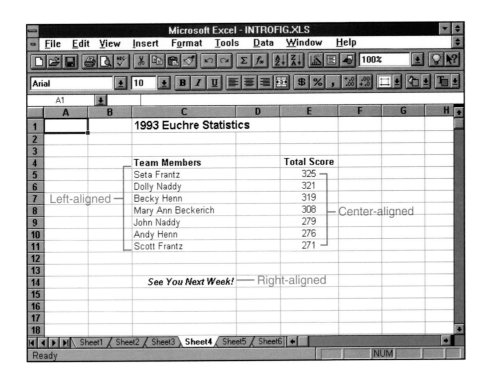

LEARNING THE LINGO

Alignment: Alignment is the way data is positioned within a cell.

Orientation: Orientation is the direction in which the characters of the text are displayed.

ALIGNING DATA IN CELLS

Aligning Data

1 Move to the cell for which you want to set alignment.

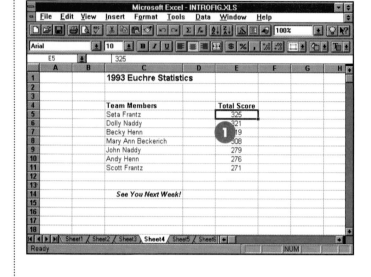

2 Click on the Format menu or press **Alt+O**.

3 Click on the Cells command or press **E**.

4 Click on the Alignment tab.

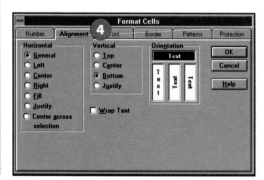

76

5 (Optional) Select the option button next to the vertical alignment you want.

6 Select **OK**, or press **Enter**.

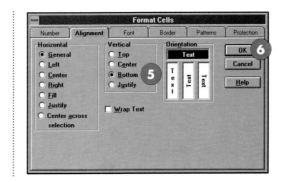

Quick Alignment

To set a cell's alignment even more quickly, just click on the appropriate alignment button in the Standard toolbar.

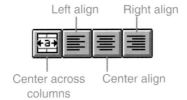

Left align   Right align

Center across columns   Center align

Editing and Formatting a Worksheet

CHANGING CELL WIDTHS

Why Adjust Cell Width?

When you type data that's too wide for a cell, Excel displays the data in one of two ways. If the data is text, and the neighboring cell is empty, Excel lets the text over-run the borders of the cell. However, if the neighboring cell is not empty, Excel cannot allow it to be covered. In this case, Excel displays only the text that fits. If the long data is a number, Excel displays a series of pound signs (**########**), which tells you that the value is too large. In either case, you'll want to widen the cell so that all its data can be displayed.

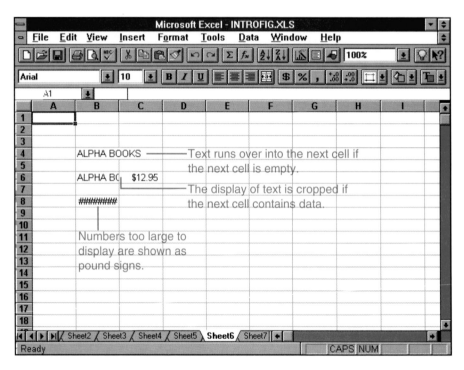

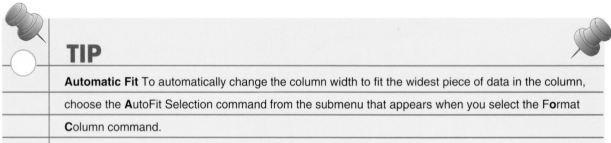

TIP

Automatic Fit To automatically change the column width to fit the widest piece of data in the column, choose the **A**utoFit Selection command from the submenu that appears when you select the **Fo**rmat **C**olumn command.

Changing a Column's Width

1 Move to any cell in the column to change.

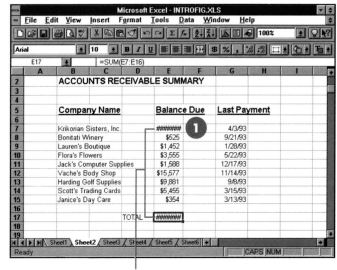

These numbers are too large to fit in their cells.

2 Click on the **Format** menu or press **Alt+O**.

3 Click on the **Column** command or press **C**.

4 Click on the **Width** command or press **W**.

5 Type the column width you desire in the Column Width text box.

6 Select **OK**, or press **Enter**.

TIP

Mousing Around Mouse users can quickly select the best fit by double-clicking the right edge of the column heading (the button containing the column letter). Or you can drag the right edge of the column heading to adjust the width manually.

CHANGING FONTS
AND TEXT ATTRIBUTES

Why Use Different Fonts and Attributes?

While Excel's default fonts and text attributes are usually acceptable for most cells in a worksheet, you may want to call attention to cells containing titles, labels, and other significant data by displaying them with different lettering. Excel can display text using any Windows font. In addition, you can assign one or more of three text attributes (bold, italic, and underlined) to text. All of these features are available from Excel's Format menu.

	A	B	C	D	E	F	G	H	I
2		ACCOUNTS RECEIVABLE SUMMARY							
3							12-point type		
4									
5		Company Name			Balance Due		Last Payment		
6									
7		Krikorian Sisters, Inc.			$1,234		4/3/93		
8		Bonitati Winery			$525		9/21/93		
9		Lauren's Boutique			$1,452		1/28/93		
10		Flora's Flowers			$3,555		5/22/93		
11		Jack's Computer Supplies			$1,588		12/17/93 — 10-point type		
12		Vache's Body Shop			$15,577		11/14/93		
13		Harding Golf Supplies			$9,881		9/8/93		
14		Scott's Trading Cards			$5,455		3/15/93		
15		Janice's Day Care			$354		3/13/93		
16									
17			TOTAL		$39,621				
18									
19									

LEARNING THE LINGO

Font: A set of characters, all of which belong to the same design family.

Text Styles: Attributes such as bold, italic, and underlining that can be applied to text.

CHANGING FONTS AND TEXT ATTRIBUTES

Changing Fonts and Attributes

1 Move to the cell for which you want to change the font.

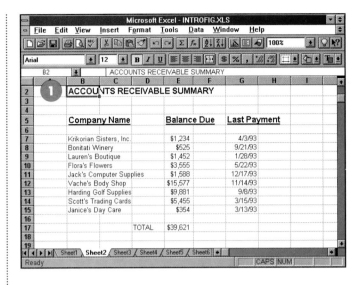

2 Click on the Format menu or press **Alt+O**.

3 Click on the Cells command or press **E**.

4 Choose the font you want from the Font list.

5 Choose the text attributes you want from the Font Style box.

6 Choose the lettering size you want from the Size box.

7 Select **OK**, or press **Enter**.

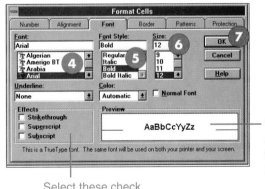

View a sample of the current font and styles here.

Select these check boxes for additional text effects.

Editing and Formatting a Worksheet

CHANGING FONTS AND TEXT ATTRIBUTES

You can also select the bold, italic, and underline font styles, as well as increase or decrease the font size, and select the font by clicking on the appropriate buttons in the Formatting toolbar.

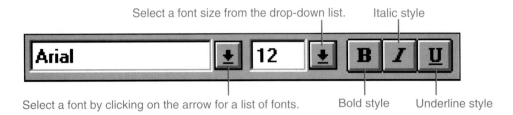

Select a font size from the drop-down list.   Italic style

Select a font by clicking on the arrow for a list of fonts.   Bold style   Underline style

Excel has many predefined formatting styles built-in that you can choose from so you don't have to format your own text. To select a predefined format, select the Auto Format command from the Format menu. From the AutoFormat dialog box, select a style from the Table Format list. A sample of the format will appear in the Sample area of the dialog box. When you have selected a style you like, select the OK button.

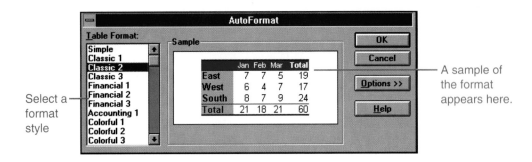

Select a format style

A sample of the format appears here.

PART 4

Printing a Worksheet

This part describes various ways to print your worksheets, something you might want to do for several reasons. You might, for example, want to use a printed copy of a worksheet in a presentation, or maybe you need "hard copy" you can refer to without starting your computer. When you have finished this part, you will be able to select a printer, set up pages, use print preview, print all or part of a worksheet, and add headers and footers to your worksheets.

- Selecting a Printer

- Printing an Entire Worksheet

- Printing Part of a Worksheet

- Using Print Preview

- Setting Up Pages

- Using Page Breaks

- Adding Headers and Footers

SELECTING A PRINTER

Why Select a Printer?

Before printing a worksheet, you must tell Excel what printer to use. If your system has only one printer connected to it, that printer is probably already selected for you. However, it's still a good idea to check before attempting to print a worksheet. Otherwise, you could waste a lot of time and paper. You can easily select a printer by using the File menu's Print command.

Selecting a Printer

1 Click on the File menu or press **Alt+F**.

2 Click on the Print command or press **P**.

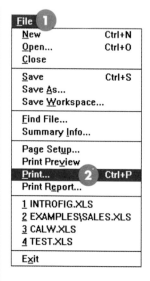

3 Select the Printer setup button.

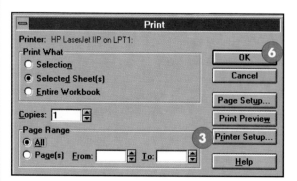

4 Select the printer you want to use from the Printer list.

5 Click on **OK**, or press **Enter**.

6 Click on **OK**, or press **Enter**.

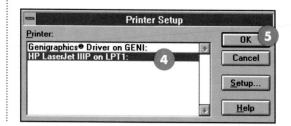

PRINTING AN ENTIRE WORKSHEET OR WORKBOOK

The Easiest Way to Print

The easiest way to print a worksheet is to print the entire sheet and let Excel worry about fitting it on the pages. If your worksheet is small, it can probably fit on one page. If your worksheet is too large to fit on a single page, Excel divides the worksheet into page-sized pieces, both vertically and horizontally. Excel then prints each piece on its own page, after which you can assemble the pieces with scissors and tape. If you want to print an entire workbook, Excel will print each worksheet on its own page.

Printing an Entire Worksheet

1 Click on the **File** menu, or press **Alt+F**.

2 Click on the **Print** command or press **P**.

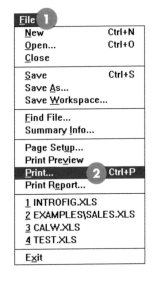

3 Select either the Selecte**d** Sheet(s) or **E**ntire Workbook option buttons.

4 Click on **OK**, or press **Enter**.

Click here to print a worksheet(s).

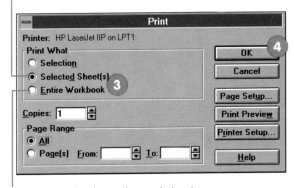

Click here to print the entire worksheet.

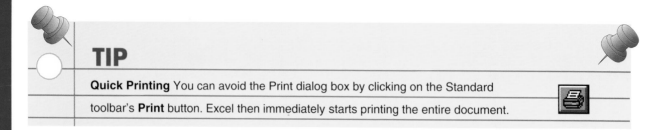

TIP

Quick Printing You can avoid the Print dialog box by clicking on the Standard

toolbar's **Print** button. Excel then immediately starts printing the entire document.

Forcing a Page

You can force the worksheet to fit on a certain number of pages by manipulating the settings in the Page Setup dialog box. Select the Page Setup button from the Print dialog box after step 2, then change the Scaling to fit to a certain number of pages. This option adjusts the font size of the printout until it fits on the specified number of pages.

Select this button...

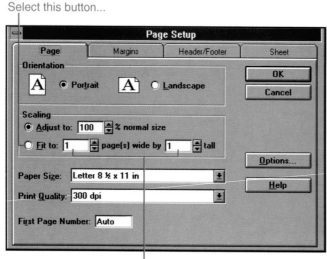

...then indicate the number of pages
in which to fit the worksheet.

PRINTING PART OF A WORKSHEET

Why Print Part of a Worksheet?

Often, you need to print only a small portion of your worksheet. For example, suppose you have a worksheet containing sales records for a group of employees, with each employee having her own table. When you're interested in printing the record for a specific employee, there's no point in printing the entire worksheet. Simply select the range of cells you want to print.

Printing Part of a Worksheet

1 Select the range that you want to print.

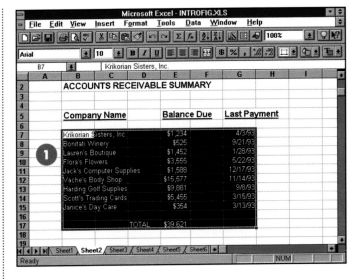

2 Click on the **F**ile menu or press **Alt+F**.

3 Click on the **P**rint command or press **P**.

PRINTING PART OF A WORKSHEET

4 Click on the Selection option button or press **Alt+N**.

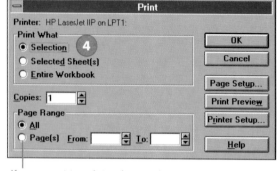

If you want to print only certain pages, select this button and enter the From and To page numbers.

5 Click on the **OK** button or press **Enter**.

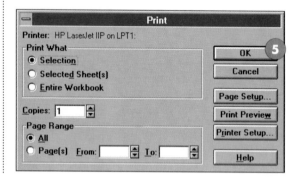

Why Use Print Preview?

There's nothing quite so frustrating as printing a document only to discover that it didn't come out the way you expected. Experimenting with layouts by printing documents is time consuming, expensive, and wastes paper. So before printing a document, make it a habit to check the layout with Print Preview.

Using Print Preview

1 Click on the **File** menu or press **Alt+F**.

2 Click on the Print Preview command or press **V**.

3 (Optional) To see the next page of your worksheet, select **Next**.

4 (Optional) To see a previous page of your worksheet, select **Previous**.

5 (Optional) To see part of the worksheet in greater detail, select **Zoom**, or click the magnifying-glass cursor on the worksheet.

6 (Optional) To print the worksheet from Print Preview, select **Print**.

7 When you're finished, select **Close**.

Select to change any of the printer setup options.

Select to change margins.

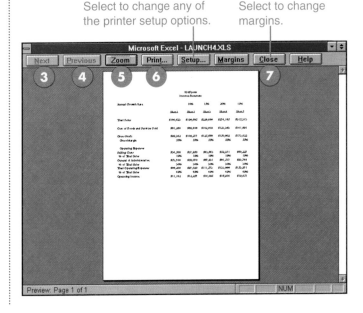

Printing a Worksheet

USING PRINT PREVIEW

Changing Margins

If your worksheet needs fine tuning before printing, you can adjust page margins and column widths right in Print Preview. Just select the **M**argins button. Sizing handles then appear on your worksheet. Drag the handles with your mouse to adjust the layout of your worksheet.

Click the Margins button to display the sizing handles.

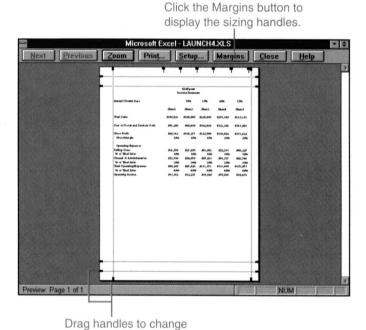

Drag handles to change margins and column widths.

TIP

Quick Print Preview To quickly preview your worksheets,

click on the **Print Preview** button on the Standard toolbar.

Why Create Page Setups?

While printing a worksheet with the default page setup is the easiest way to get your data on paper, if you have special needs, you can modify the page setup any way you like. Using Excel's Page Setup dialog box, you can change page orientation, paper size, margins, scaling, headers and footers, and other options that control how your finished printout looks.

Select this tab to adjust the margins.

Select this tab to add or edit a header or footer.

Select this tab to select the way worksheets are printed.

Portrait is the normal orientation. Lanscape prints sideways.

Here you can scale the size of the printer worksheet image.

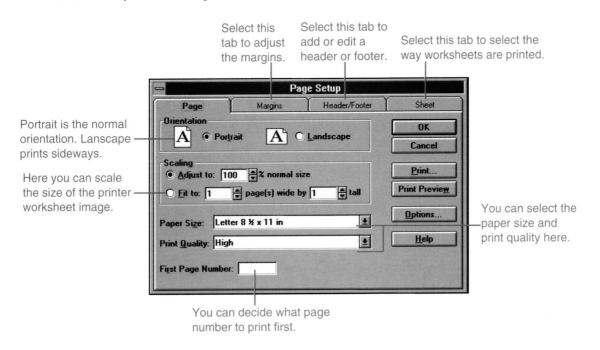

You can select the paper size and print quality here.

You can decide what page number to print first.

LEARNING THE LINGO

Scaling: Scaling means to reduce or enlarge the size of your worksheet's image. For example, to print a worksheet at half its normal size, you'd reduce it by 50%. To print your worksheet twice as large, you'd enlarge it by 200%.

Printing a Worksheet

Setting Up Pages

1 Click on the File menu or press **F**.

2 Click on the Page Setup command or press **U**.

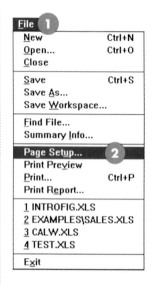

3 Change any of the page setup options you need to change.

4 (Optional) To change the margins of the page(s), select the **Margins** tab and change as needed.

5 (Optional) To add or edit a header or footer, select the **Header/Footer** tab and change as needed.

6 (Optional) To change the order of the worksheets to print or add gridlines, select the **Sheet** tab and make changes as needed.

7 When complete, click on the **OK** button or press **Enter**.

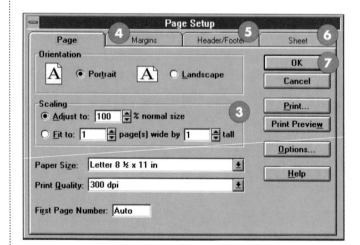

Why Insert Page Breaks?

If you want sections of a worksheet to appear on specific pages, you can move those sections to new columns and rows in order to make them appear on the page you want. However, an easier way to place a worksheet section on its own page is to insert page breaks into the document. When Excel is printing a document and sees a page break, it automatically ejects the current page from the printer and starts a new one.

When you set a page break, Excel places a break to the left of the current cell and a break above the current cell. Other pages in the document are readjusted to reflect the new page layout.

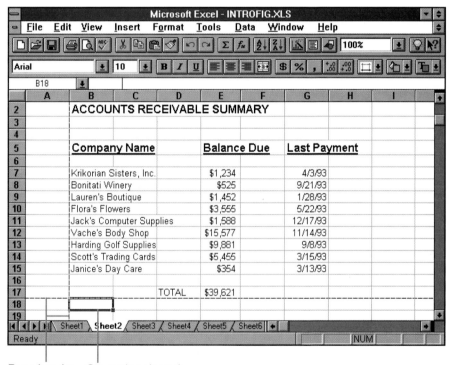

Page breaks   Currently selected

USING PAGE BREAKS

Your worksheet can have two kinds of page breaks. *Automatic page breaks* are included automatically by Excel, based on the settings in the Page Setup dialog box. *Manual page breaks* are the ones you add with the Insert Page Break command. How can you tell them apart? In an automatic page break, the dashes that make up the page-break line are shorter than those in a manual page break.

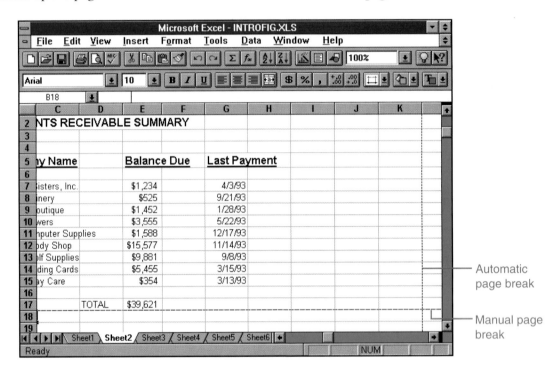

LEARNING THE LINGO

Page break: A page break is a marker that tells Excel where to eject the current page from the printer and start a new one. Excel automatically places page breaks to divide a worksheet into page-sized pieces. However, you can add your own page breaks and so force Excel to organize the printout the way you want it to be organized.

Inserting Page Breaks

1 Move to the cell where you want the page break inserted.

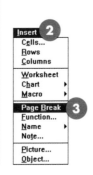

2 Click on the Insert menu or press **Alt+I**.

3 Click on the Set Page **B**reak command or press **B**.

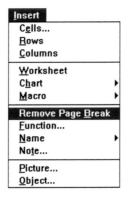

Deleting a Page Break

To delete a page break, move to the cell immediately below and to the right of the page break you want to delete. Then select Remove Page **B**reak from the Insert menu.

Printing a Worksheet

ADDING HEADERS AND FOOTERS

Why Use Headers and Footers?

Headers and footers allow you to print page numbers, file descriptions, and other information on every page of a printout. Headers are printed at the top of the page, and footers are printed at the bottom. To help you construct headers and footers, Excel includes special codes that represent page numbers, date and time stamps, and file names in your headers and footers. In addition, you can specify font types and sizes.

The Header and Footer dialog box lets you specify which header elements to print at three positions: left, center, and right. Any text you type in a section appears as part of the header. In addition, the dialog box's buttons give you quick access to the codes you need to add pages numbers, dates, and other common header and footer elements.

Sample of what the selected header will look like.

Select predefined header/footer from drop-down lists.

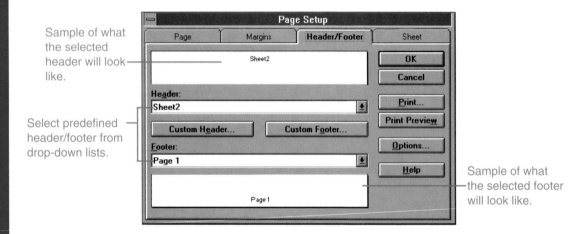

Sample of what the selected footer will look like.

You create headers and footers in exactly the same way. The only difference is where they're printed on the page.

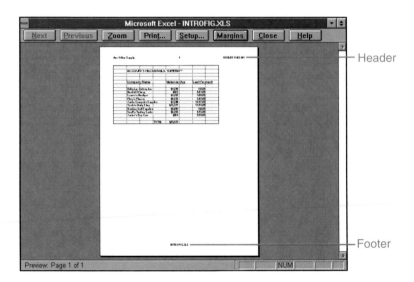

Header

Footer

Adding Header and Footers

1 Click on the **File** menu or press **Alt+F**.

2 Click on the Page Set**u**p command or press **U**.

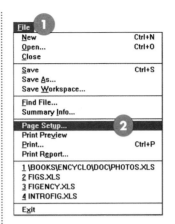

3 Select the **Header/Footer** tab from the Page Setup dialog box.

4 (Optional) Select a predefined header from the Header drop down list.

5 (Optional) Select a predefined footer from the Footer drop down list.

6 (Optional) If you want to create your own header or footer, select the Custom Header or Custom Footer buttons.

7 Click in the **L**eft, **C**enter, or **R**ight edit box sections and type the text you would like to appear in these sections of the header.

8 Click on any of the buttons to insert a page number, date, time filename, or tab name in the edit boxes.

9 Click on the **OK** button or press **Enter**.

10 Click on the **OK** button or press **Enter**.

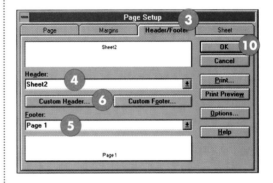

Select a font · Insert page number of total pages · Insert time

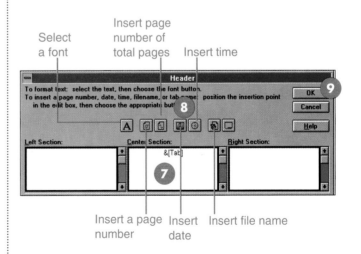

Insert a page number · Insert date · Insert file name

ADDING HEADERS AND FOOTERS

Exercise

Load a worksheet you have already created or type the data from the worksheet in the figure and then add a header.

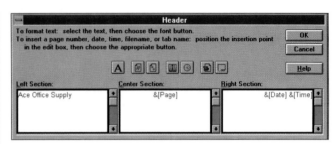

1 Select Page Setup from the File menu.

2 Select the Custom Header button.

3 In the Left Section box, type **Ace Office Supply**.

4 Click in the Center Section box to move the cursor there and then click on the **Insert Page Number** button.

5 Click in the Right Section box to move the cursor there and then click on the **date** button, type a space, and then click on the **time** button.

6 Click on the **OK** button or press **Enter**.

7 Click on the **OK** button or press **Enter**.

8 Go to Print Preview to see the header you created.

PART 5

CHARTING DATA IN A WORKSHEET

This part describes how to display worksheet data in chart form. Because charts are often easier to understand than long lists of numbers, you can easily evaluate portions of your worksheets as a chart. When you have finished this part, you will be able to create several types of charts; delete charts; edit charts; and add labels, notes, and legends to charts.

- Creating a Chart with ChartWizard
- Changing a Chart's Type
- Giving a Chart Its Own Window
- Editing a Chart with ChartWizard
- Changing Values on a Chart
- Adding a Chart Legend
- Deleting Chart Elements
- Deleting an Embedded Chart

CREATING A CHART WITH CHARTWIZARD

What Is ChartWizard?

Creating a chart can be a meticulous process, but Excel provides a special tool called *ChartWizard* that does much of the chart-creating work for you. ChartWizard guides you every step of the way through the creation of your chart, making it possible to design a sophisticated chart with only a few mouse clicks. You start ChartWizard by clicking its button on Excel's Standard toolbar.

Creating a Chart with Chart Wizard

1 Move to the upper left corner of the block you want to convert to a chart.

2 Holding down the left mouse button, drag the mouse pointer to the lower right corner of the block.

3 Click on the **ChartWizard** button in Excel's Standard toolbar.

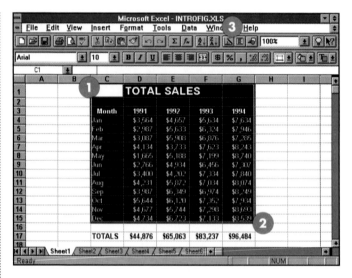

4 Click where you want the upper left corner of the chart to be, and then drag the mouse pointer in order to outline the size of the chart.

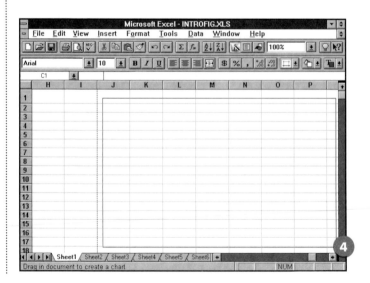

100

5 Select **Next**.

6 Click on the chart type you want, and then select **Next**.

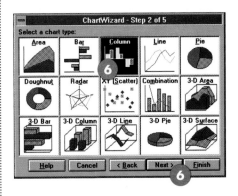

7 Click on the chart format you want, and select **Next**.

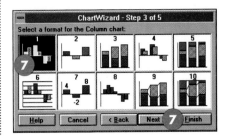

8 Select options until the sample chart appears they way you want yours to look, and then select **Next**.

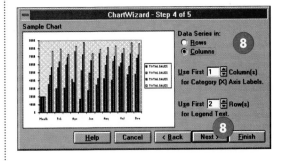

9 Select Yes or No to choose whether a legend will be used.

10 (Optional) Type a title under Chart Title.

11 Select the Finish button.

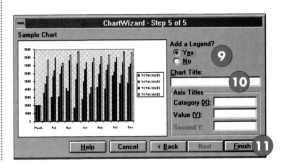

Charting Data in a Worksheet

CREATING A CHART WITH CHARTWIZARD

Adding Labels

When you highlight a block of data for a chart, include the data's labels, and
ChartWizard will automatically add the labels to the chart.

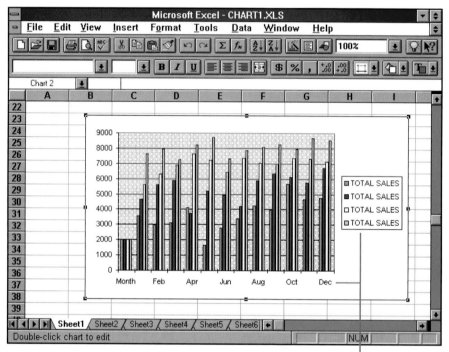

These labels were copied from the worksheet.

LEARNING THE LINGO

Legend: A chart legend tells you what the different parts
of a chart mean.

Exercise

In this exercise, you'll create a simple worksheet and then create a bar chart from the data.

1 Enter the data shown in the figure.

2 Click on cell **B3**.

3 Holding down the left mouse button, drag the mouse pointer down to **C15**.

4 Click on the **ChartWizard** button in Excel's toolbar.

5 Click on cell **E4**, and, holding down the left mouse button, drag the mouse pointer to cell **I16**.

6 Select **Next** in the Step 1 dialog box.

7 Select **Next** in the Step 2 dialog box.

8 Select **Next** in the Step 3 dialog box.

9 Select **Next** in the Step 4 dialog box.

10 In the Step 5 dialog box, click on **No** for a chart legend, and then select the **F**inish button.

11 Save the worksheet to use in later exercises. Use the file name **SAVED.XLS**.

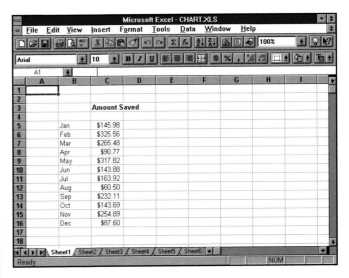

Chart toolbar

Charting Data in a Worksheet

CHANGING A CHART'S TYPE

Why Change the Chart Type?

Once you've created your chart with ChartWizard, the Chart toolbox appears with charting buttons. This toolbox contains buttons to help you edit your charts. By using the buttons in the toolbox, you can change the chart you have created any way you like. While the chart is on the screen, you might, for example, want to experiment with different chart types, to see which type best displays the data. Changing the chart type is so easy, you should switch among many types until you find the type best suited to your needs.

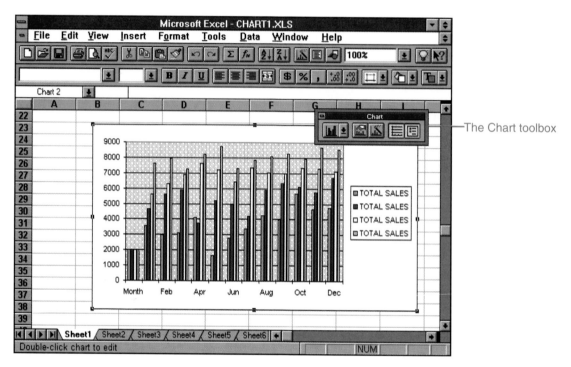

The Chart toolbox

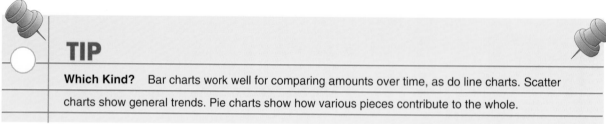

TIP

Which Kind?   Bar charts work well for comparing amounts over time, as do line charts. Scatter charts show general trends. Pie charts show how various pieces contribute to the whole.

Changing a Chart's Type

1 Click on the chart to select it.

2 In the Chart toolbox, click on the down arrow of the Chart Type button to display a list of chart types.

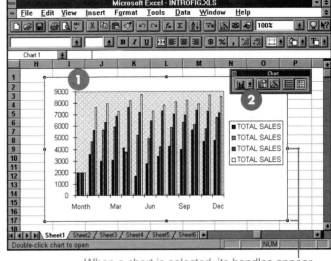

When a chart is selected, its handles appear.

3 Click on a chart type of your choice.

Click on	To Create	Click on	To Create
	area chart		3D area chart
	bar chart		3D bar chart
	column bar chart		3D column bar chart
	line chart		3D line chart
	pie chart		3D pie chart
	scatter chart		3D surface chart
	doughnut chart		3D radar chart

Charting Data in a Worksheet

GIVING A CHART ITS OWN WINDOW

Why Give a Chart Its Own Window?

Excel's ChartWizard tool creates *embedded charts*, charts which are part of the worksheet. You cannot save these charts independently of the worksheet, and there are limitations on the editing you can perform on them. Chart worksheets or documents, on the other hand, are charts that have their own windows or sheets that can be saved to their own files and edited using a full range of tools and commands.

Creating a Separate Chart Worksheet

1 Click on the Insert menu or press **Alt+I**.

2 Click on the **C**hart command or press **H**.

3 Click on the **As** New Sheet command or press **A**.

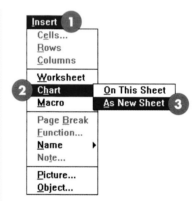

4 Create the chart you want using the ChartWizard dialog boxes that appear, and click on the Finish button when you are done.

LEARNING THE LINGO

Embedded chart: An embedded chart is part of a worksheet.

EDITING A CHART WITH CHARTWIZARD

When Would I Edit a Chart?

As you add data to a worksheet, you may also find that you need to add the data to your charts. Just as you used ChartWizard to create the charts, you can also use ChartWizard to edit the charts' contents. Using ChartWizard, you can add new data to the chart or change the way the data is displayed.

Editing a Chart with ChartWizard

1 Click on the chart you want to edit.

2 Click on the **ChartWizard** button on the Chart toolbox.

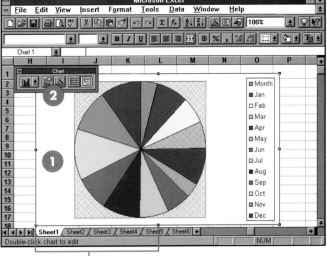

When you click on the chart, these selection handles appear.

3 Edit the **Range** to include any new data you want in the chart.

4 Click on the **Next** button.

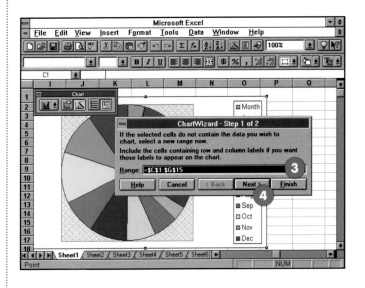

107

EDITING A CHART WITH CHARTWIZARD

5 Click on the display options to create the type of chart you want.

6 When completed editing the chart, click on the **OK** button.

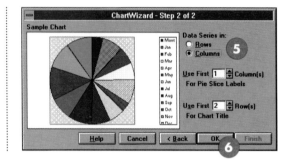

Exercise

Load the worksheet and chart named **SAVED.XLS** that you created in the first task in this part. Then add the second column of data shown in the figure here. (You can use whatever numbers you like.) Then follow the steps in this exercise to add the new data to the chart.

1 Click on the chart.

2 On the chart toolbox, click on the **ChartWizard** button.

3 In the Range text box, change the range to **$B$3:$D$16**, and then click on the **Next** button.

4 In the Step 2 dialog box, select **OK**.

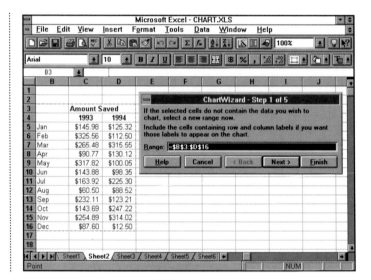

TIP

Drag and Plot   To quickly add chart data to a chart, select the data from the worksheet and drag it onto the chart. You will get the **Paste Special** dialog box. Make the necessary (or desired) selections and select **OK**. The chart will be updated with the new data.

CHANGING VALUES ON A CHART

Why Change Values?

Worksheets are often used to perform projections on data to see what might happen if a certain situation occurred. One way to experiment with values in this way is to simply change the cells in the worksheet to see how the change affects other cells. However, if the data with which you want to experiment is also displayed in a chart, you can use your mouse to modify the chart, which also changes the associated values in the worksheet.

Changing Data Values on a Chart

1   To select the chart, double-click anywhere in the chart.

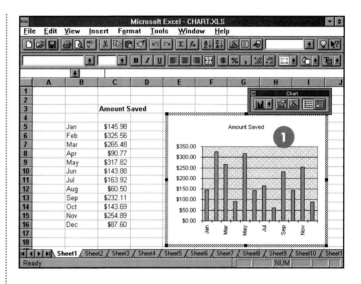

2   Click on the top of the data marker you want to change.

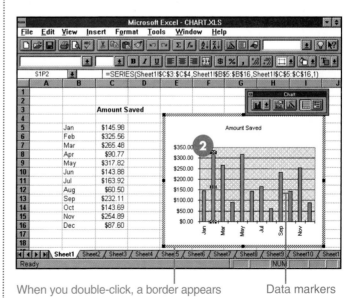

When you double-click, a border appears around the chart to indicate that you can edit it.

Data markers

CHANGING VALUES ON A CHART

3 Drag the data marker to its new position.

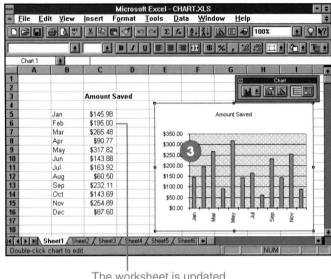

The worksheet is updated with the new value.

LEARNING THE LINGO

Data marker: A data marker represents a value in a chart. For example, in a bar chart, the data markers are the bars, whereas in a pie chart, the data markers are the pie slices.

ADDING A CHART LEGEND

Why Use Legends?

Legends are another element you can use to make a chart more understandable and are especially important when a chart displays multiple data series. When ChartWizard creates a chart with multiple data series, it plots each data series in its own color. The legend then shows which color goes with which data series, information that can be critical in order to correctly interpret the chart.

Adding a Chart Legend

1 Type column titles on the worksheet.

2 Click on the chart to select it.

3 Click on the **Legend** button in the Chart toolbox.

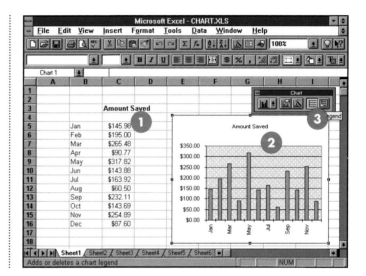

LEARNING THE LINGO

Data series: A data series in a chart is equivalent to a column of data in a worksheet. For example, a chart created from a two-column table will usually have two data series, each plotted with its own color.

Charting Data in a Worksheet

DELETING CHART ELEMENTS

Why Delete Chart Elements?

As you experiment with different chart layouts, you may want to delete elements that don't work quite right for your purposes. Deleting chart elements, such as titles and legends, is as easy as selecting an element and pressing the keyboard's Delete key. When you delete a chart element, you completely remove it from the chart.

Deleting Chart Elements

1 To select the chart, double-click anywhere in the chart.

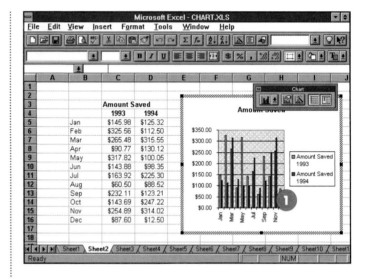

2 Click on the chart element you want to delete.

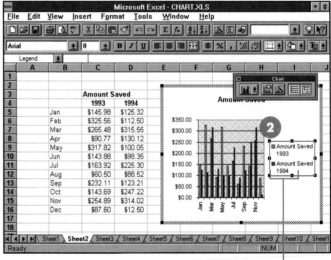

When a chart element is selected, its handles appear.

3 Press the keyboard's **Delete** key.

DELETING AN EMBEDDED CHART

Why Delete a Chart?

As your worksheets evolve, you may no longer need to chart certain blocks of data. Having extraneous charts cluttering up your worksheet not only wastes worksheet space, but also makes the worksheet harder to understand. To keep your worksheets concise, you should delete old charts as soon as they're no longer needed.

Deleting an Embedded Chart

1 Click on the chart you want to delete.

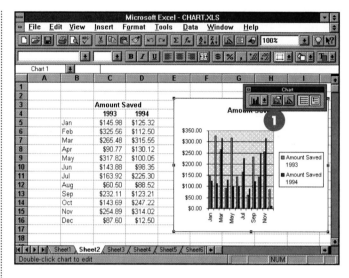

2 Press **Delete**.

TIP

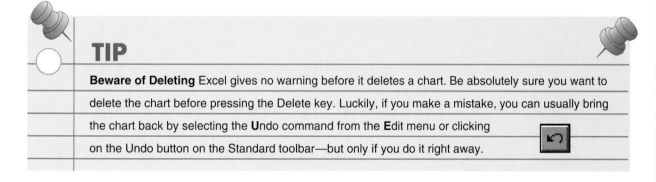

Beware of Deleting Excel gives no warning before it deletes a chart. Be absolutely sure you want to delete the chart before pressing the Delete key. Luckily, if you make a mistake, you can usually bring the chart back by selecting the **U**ndo command from the **E**dit menu or clicking on the Undo button on the Standard toolbar—but only if you do it right away.

Charting Data in a Worksheet

PART 6

Automating Your Work

When working in Excel, you may need to perform the same tasks or enter the same data over and over again. Excel provides a *macro* feature which lets you record your actions and repeat them when needed, therefore, saving you time and effort. When you finish this part, you will know how to record, play back, and delete a macro and assign your most frequently used macros to a menu.

- Recording a Macro
- Running a Macro
- Deleting a Macro
- Assigning a Macro to a Menu

RECORDING A MACRO

What Is a Macro?

A *macro* is a series of commands that you can record and save. You can then play back these commands at any time allowing you to automate your work. For example, to save a file and then print it, you can choose the **S**ave command from the File menu, select the **P**rint command from the File menu, and then select the **OK** button. However, you can simply record all of these steps in a macro and then play them back (run the macro) in a single step.

Macro name

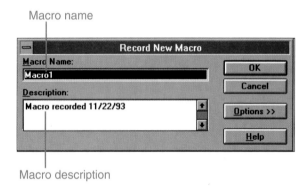

Macro description

LEARNING THE LINGO

Macro: A macro is used to save work and time by recording commands or tasks that can be played back at a later time to automate your work.

Recording a Macro

1 Select the **T**ools menu, or press **Alt+T**.

2 Select the **R**ecord Macro command, or press **R**.

3 Select the **R**ecord New Macro command, or press **R**.

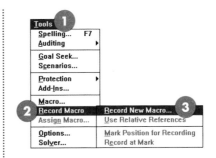

4 Type the name of the macro you want to record in the **M**acro Name text box.

5 (Optional) Type a description of the macro in the **D**escription box.

6 Select the **OK** button. The Stop Macro button appears in its own toolbar.

7 Perform the actions you want to record in the order you want them recorded.

8 Click on the **Stop Macro** button on the Macro toolbar on the screen, or select the **T**ools **R**ecord Macro **S**top Recording command.

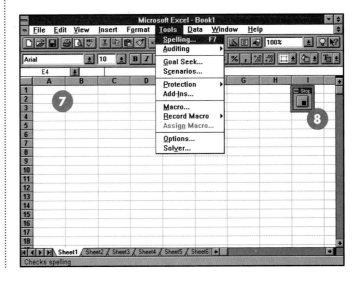

Automating Your Work

RECORDING A MACRO

Exercise

To practice recording a macro, record a macro which assigns bold, italic, and center formatting to a cell(s).

1 Select the **T**ools menu, or press **Alt+T**.

2 Select the **R**ecord Macro command, or press **R**.

3 Select the **R**ecord New Macro command, or press **R**.

4 Type **BOLD** in the **M**acro Name text box.

5 Type **Bold, Italic, and Center** in the **D**escription text box.

6 Select the **OK** button.

7 Click on the **Bold**, **Italic**, and **Center** buttons on the Formatting toolbar.

8 Click on the **Stop Macro** button on the Macro floating toolbar.

How Do You Run a Recorded Macro?

Once you have recorded a set of commands or tasks in a macro, you can run that macro as many times as needed in Excel.

Recorded macros

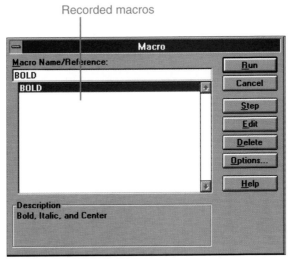

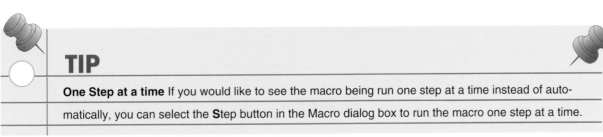

TIP

One Step at a time If you would like to see the macro being run one step at a time instead of automatically, you can select the **S**tep button in the Macro dialog box to run the macro one step at a time.

Running a Macro

1 Select the Tools menu, or press **Alt+T**.

2 Select the Macro command, or press **M**.

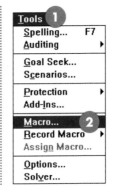

RUNNING A MACRO

3 Select the macro you want to run from the list of recorded macros, or type the name of the macro in the **M**acro Name/Reference text box.

4 Select the **R**un button, or press **Enter**.

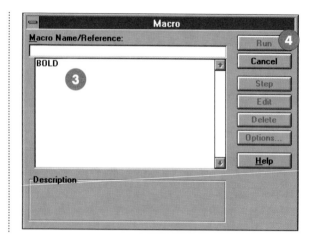

TIP

STOP! If you accidentally ran the wrong macro or just want to stop the macro after it has begun to run, press the **Esc** key.

Exercise

To practice running a macro, run the macro you recorded in the previous task called **BOLD**.

1 Select the cell(s) you want to apply bold, italic, and center formatting to.

2 Select the **T**ools menu, or press **Alt+T**.

3 Select the **M**acro command, or press **M**.

4 Select the **BOLD** macro from the list of available macros.

5 Select the **R**un button, or press **Enter**.

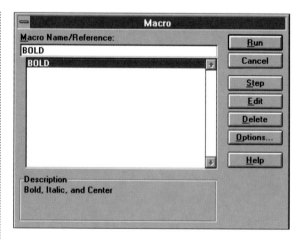

Why Delete a Macro?

If you find that you no longer need a macro or have made a mistake in a macro and want to start all over, Excel allows you to delete any unwanted macros.

If you need to look at a macro or edit it, select the Edit button from the Macro dialog box. The macro appears in a window so you can see or edit the commands or codes. For more information on how to edit your macro, see the Excel manual on editing visual basic code (this is the language the macro is written in).

Deleting a Macro

1 Select the Tools menu, or press **Alt+T**.

2 Select the **M**acro command, or press **M**.

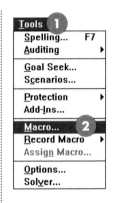

3 Select the macro you want to delete from the list of recorded macros, or type the name of the macro in the **M**acro Name/Reference text box.

4 Select the **D**elete button or press **Alt+D**.

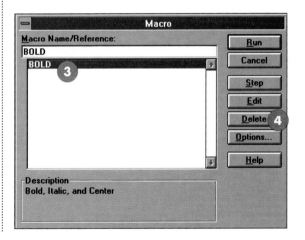

ASSIGNING A MACRO TO A MENU

Why Assign a Macro to a Menu?

If you have recorded a macro that you use on a regular basis, you can speed up your work further by adding that macro to the Tools menu. Not only does it speed up your work, but it makes it easier for you to run your important macros. Once you add a macro to the Tools menu, you can select the macro to run the same way you access any menu command in Excel.

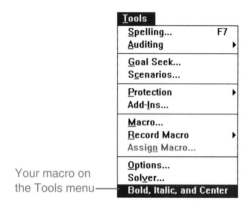

Your macro on the Tools menu

Assigning a Macro to the Tools Menu

1. Select the Tools menu, or press **Alt+T**.

2. Select the **Macro** command, or press **M**.

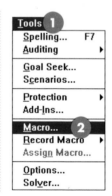

3 Select the macro you want to assign to the **T**ools menu from the list of recorded macros or type the name of the macro in the **M**acro Name/Reference text box.

4 Select the **O**ptions button, or press **Alt+O**.

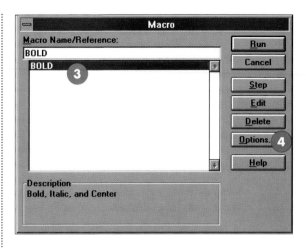

5 Select the Men**u** Item on Tools Menu check box, or press **Alt+U**.

6 Type the command name as you want it to appear on the **T**ools menu.

7 Select the **OK** button, or press **Enter**.

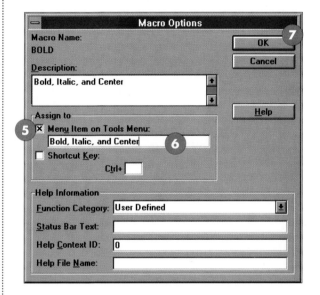

8 Select the **Close** button in the Macro dialog box.

Automating Your Work

Installing Excel

When you first open Excel's package, you'll find that the program is shipped on five high-density floppy disks. Before you can use Excel, you must install it onto your computer. In most cases, installation is automatic, with your needing to do little more than answer a few questions and swap disks when prompted. Although Excel offers a custom installation that lets you select what portions of the program to install, unless you're sure of what you're doing, you should use the automated installation described here.

The installation instructions here assume you'll install Excel from drive A. If you need to use drive B, just substitute B for A in the instructions.

QUICK REFRESHER

If you have a mouse, you'll want to use it for the installation. The skills you'll need are:

- **Point:** To move the mouse on its pad until the on-screen pointer points at the desired object.

- **Click:** To press and release the left mouse button once. When you "click on" an object, you first point to it and then click.

- **Double-click:** To press and release the left mouse button twice quickly.

If you're a keyboard-only user, you'll need to use some key combinations to complete the installation. When you see two keys written with a plus sign between them, such as **Alt+C**, it means you should hold down the first key and then press the second key.

Installing Excel

1. Start your computer, and type **WIN** to run Windows.

2. Insert Excel's disk #1 into drive A.

3 If you don't see the Program
Manager window, double-click
on the icon labelled **Program
Manager** to open it.

If you see "Program Manager"
in the title bar, it's already open.

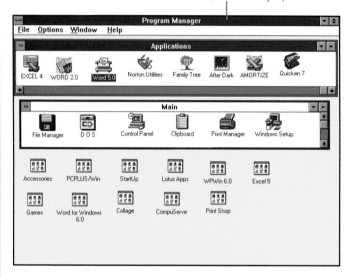

4 Click on **File** at the top left corner of the screen, or hold
down the **Alt** key, and press **F**.

5 Click on the **Run** command, or
press **R**.

6 Type **a:setup**, or **b:setup**, and
press **Enter**.

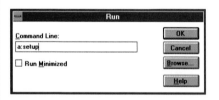

7 To begin installing, press Enter.

126

8 If you want to install Excel on drivveC:, click on Continue, or press **Alt + C**. Otherwise, type the drive and directory in the Install to box before selecting Continue.

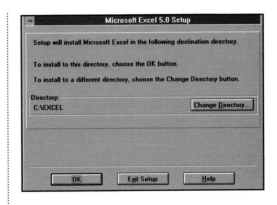

9 Click on the **Typical** button, or press **Enter**.

10 Select a program group from the **E**xisting Groups list or enter a new group name in the **P**rogram Group text box and select the **C**ontinue button.

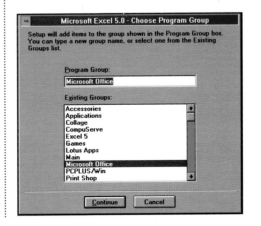

11 When you are prompted, place the requested disk into drive A or B, and pre

12 Repeat step 11 until Excel is fully installed.

13 When Excel completely installs, click on **OK**, or press **Enter**.

Glossary

Alignment   Alignment is the way data is positioned within a cell.

Arguments   The values functions need in order to calculate a result. A function's arguments are enclosed in parentheses.

Attached Text   Text that is connected to a particular chart element.

Axis   A chart has two axes: the Y axis usually displays data values, and the X axis usually displays data categories.

Cell   A cell is a small box at the intersection of a row and column in the worksheet. Each cell can hold a single piece of data or a formula.

Cell cursor   The cell cursor is a dark box that surrounds the current cell.

Cell format   A cell's format is the way a cell displays its data, including the number type, the alignment of data within the cell, and text styles, such as bold or italics.

Cell range   A cell range refers to a block of cells and consists of two cell references separated by a colon.

Cell reference   A column letter followed by a row number that refers to the value in a particular cell.

Chart document   A chart document is not part of a worksheet and has its own window.

Check marks   A check mark next to a menu option means the option is currently selected.

Click   Press and release the left mouse button.

Column   A column is a vertical line of cells, each identified by a letter.

Command button   An on-screen button object that you can click to select a specific Excel command.

Data marker   A data marker represents a value in a chart. For example, in a bar chart, the data markers are the bars, whereas in a pie chart, the data markers are the pie slices.

Data series   A data series in a chart is equivalent to a column of data in a worksheet. For example, a chart created from a two-column table will usually have two data series, each plotted with its own color.

Directory   Directories are like little file cabinets on your hard drive that help you organize your files. They can contain either files or other directories.

Double-click   Press and release the left mouse button twice quickly.

GLOSSARY

Drag Point to a screen object and then hold down the left mouse button while you move the mouse, dragging the pointer across the screen.

Ellipsis An ellipsis is three dots (...). When an ellipsis follows a menu command, the command displays a dialog box when selected.

Embedded chart An embedded chart is part of a worksheet.

File Your worksheets are stored on your hard disk in a *file*, a collection of related data stored as a single unit.

Font A set of characters, all of which belong to the same design family.

Grayed-out Grayed-out menu commands are displayed lighter than other commands and cannot be selected.

Hot keys Keystrokes you can use to instantly select a menu command.

Insertion cursor A blinking vertical bar that shows where the next typed character will appear.

Label A series of characters that have no numerical value. A label is usually used for headings and notations.

Legend A chart legend tells you what the different parts of a chart mean.

Minimized Shrunken to the size of an icon; windows that are not in use are often minimized so they do not clutter the screen.

Operator precedence The order in which arithmetic operations are performed, also called "order of operations."

Operators Excel supports many operators that you can use in your formulas, including addition (+), subtraction (-), multiplication (*), division (/), and percentage (%).

Orientation Orientation is the direction in which the characters of the text are displayed.

Page break A page break is a marker that tells Excel where to eject the current page from the printer and start a new one. Excel automatically places page breaks to divide a worksheet into page-sized pieces. However, you can add your own page breaks and so force Excel to organize the printout the way you want it to be organized.

Point Position the mouse pointer over an object on the screen.

Print area When you want to print only a section of a worksheet, you select a print area. The print area remains effective until you remove it.

Program group A window containing one or more program icons.

Program group icon A small picture representing a program group that has been minimized.

Program icon   A small picture representing a program you can run. The program name usually appears under the picture.

Row   A row is a horizontal line of cells, each identified by a number.

Scaling   Scaling means to reduce or enlarge the size of your worksheet's image. For example, to print a worksheet at half its normal size, you'd reduce it by 50%. To print your worksheet twice as large, you'd enlarge it by 200%.

Select All button   The blank button at the intersection of the column letter row and the row numbers column.

Selection letter   The underlined letter in a menu or command name.

Status Bar   An area at the bottom of Excel's main window that displays messages about the worksheet's status.

Text Styles   Attributes such as bold, italic, and underlining that can be applied to text.

Toggle   To switch an option from on to off or from off to on.

Toolbar   A stationary row of command buttons at the top or bottom of Excel's main window.

Toolbox   A small, movable box containing command buttons.

Unattached Text   Text that sits on top of the chart, unconnected to a particular element.

Workbook   Excel files are called workbooks. Each workbook consists of 16 worksheets or documents.

Worksheet functions   These are built-in functions that you can use to calculate values. Some functions are SUM, which calculates sums; AVERAGE, which calculates averages; and SQRT, which calculates square roots. There are hundreds of worksheet functions, all of which are listed in the *Function Reference* that came with your copy of Excel.

Index

Symbols

– (subtraction) operator, 47
(pound signs), values in cells, 78-79
$ (dollar sign), absolute references, 59
‘ (single quote), changing values to labels, 42
* (multiplication) operator, 47
+ (addition) operator, 47
/ (division) operator, 47
= (equals sign), entering formulas, 48
^ (exponentiation) operator, 47
… (ellipsis), 17, 130
3D charts, 105

A

absolute references, 59
active worksheet, 14
addition (+) operator, 47
addresses of cells, current, 14
alignment, 75, 129
    data in cells, 75-77
    values versus labels, 42
alphanumeric keys, 8
Alt (Alternative) key, 8
    with selection letters, 18
area charts, 105
arguments in functions, 52, 54, 129
arrow keys, 8
arrows
    after menu commands, 17
    scroll, 16
As New Sheet command (Insert Chart submenu), 106
attached text, 129

attributes, 80-82
Auto Format command (Format menu), 82
Auto Sum button, Standard Toolbar, 54
AutoFit Selection command (Format Column submenu), 78
automatic page breaks, 94
AVERAGE function, 49
axes, 129

B

bar charts, 104-105
Bold style button, Formatting Toolbar, 82
bold text, macro for, 118
buttons, 23
    command, 19, 129
        selecting, 20
    contents (help), 24
    Find File, Open dialog box, 33-34
    Formatting Toolbar, *see* Formatting Toolbar
    Formula Bar, 57
    Maximize, 16
    Minimize, 16
    option, 19
        selecting, 20
    Print Preview window, 89
    Restore, 16
    search (help), 24
    Select All, 131
    Standard Toolbar, *see* Standard Toolbar
    tab scrolling, 2, 14
    Toolbars, selecting, 21

C

calculations
    averaging, 49
    displaying results, 48
    functions, 52-54
    operator precedence, 47
cancelling macros in progress, 120
cell cursor, 2-3, 14, 38, 129
cells, 2-3, 14, 129
    addresses, current, 14
    clearing contents, 66-67
    copying, 58-61
    data
        aligning, 75-77
        editing, 56-57
        finding, 68-69
        replacing, 70
        sorting, 71-72
    entering
        dates and times, 46
        formulas, 48
        functions, 53-54
        labels, 41
        values, 44
    formats, 67, 129
    moving, 58-61
    ranges, *see* ranges
    references, 3, 49, 129
        absolute, 59
        relative, 58-59
    selecting, 38-39
    widths, changing, 78-79
Cells command (Format menu)
    Alignment tab, 76-77
    Font tab, 81
    Number tab, 46, 73-74
Center Across Columns button, Standard Toolbar, 77

Center Align button, Standard
    Toolbar, 77
center-aligned data, 75
        macro for, 118
central processing units (CPUs), 8
Chart command (Insert menu),
    As New Sheet, 106
chart documents, 106, 129
Chart Toolbox, 104
        Chart Type button, 105
        ChartWizard button, 107
        Legend button, 111
Chart Type button, Chart
    Toolbox, 105
charts
        axes, 129
        changing values for what-if
            analysis, 109-110
        creating, 100-103
        deleting elements, 112
        editing, 107-108
        embedded, 106, 130
            deleting, 113
        in separate windows, 106
        labels, 102
        legends, 111
        types, changing, 104-105
ChartWizard, 100-103, 107-108
ChartWizard button
        Chart Toolbox, 107
        Standard Toolbar, 100
check boxes, 19
        selecting, 20
check marks, 129
Clear command (Edit menu), 66
clearing cell contents, 66-67
clicking mouse, 9, 13, 129
Close command (File menu), 30
closing
        windows, 16
        workbooks, 30
column bar charts, 105
Column command (Format menu)
        AutoFit Selection, 78
        Width, 79
columns, 2, 14, 129
        changing widths, 78-79
        deleting, 64-65
        headings, 40
        inserting into worksheets,
            62-63
        selecting, 39, 62

Columns command (Insert
    menu), 63
Comma style button, Formatting
    Toolbar, 74
command buttons, 19, 129
        selecting, 20
commands
        … (ellipsis), 17, 130
        arrows after, 17
        Auto Format (Format
            menu), 82
        Cells (Format menu)
            Alignment tab, 76-77
            Font tab, 81
            Number tab, 46, 73-74
        Chart (Insert menu), As New
            Sheet, 106
        check marks, 129
        Clear (Edit menu), 66
        Close (File menu), 30
        Column (Format menu)
            AutoFit Selection, 78
            Width, 79
        Columns (Insert menu), 63
        Contents (Help menu), 24
        Delete (Edit menu), 65
        Delete Sheet (Edit menu), 65
        Exit (File menu), 35
        Find (Edit menu), 68-69
        Function (Insert menu), 53-54
        grayed-out, 17, 130
        Macro (Tools menu), 119-123
        Macro-name (Tools menu),
            122-123
        New (File menu), 29
        Open (File menu), 27-28,
            33-34
        Options (Tools menu), Edit
            tab, 57, 60
        Page Break (Insert menu), 95
        Page Setup (File menu), 92,
            97-98
        Print (File menu), 84-85,
            87-88
        Print Preview (File menu),
            89-90
        Record Macro (Tools menu)
            Record New Macro,
                117-118
            Stop Recording, 117
        Remove Page Break (Insert
            menu), 95
        Replace (Edit menu), 70

Rows (Insert menu), 63
Run (Program Manager File
    menu), 126
Save (File menu), 31
Save As (File menu), 32
selecting
        from menus, 17-18
        from Toolbars or
            Toolboxes, 21
selection letters, 17, 131
shortcut keys, 17
shortcut menu
        Clear Contents, 67
        Delete, 65
        Format Cells, 46
        Insert, 63
Sort (Data menu), 71-72
Toolbars (View menu), 22
Undo (Edit menu), 65
WIN, 12, 126
Worksheet (Insert menu), 63
computer components, 7-10
contents button (help), 24
Contents command (Help
    menu), 24
contiguous cells, 38
Control-menu box, 16, 19
Copy button, Standard Toolbar, 60
copying cells, 58-61
CPUs (central processing units), 8
Ctrl (Control) key, 8
Currency style button, Formatting
    Toolbar, 74
current cell address, 14
cursors
        cell, 2-3, 14, 38, 129
        insertion, 56, 130
Cut button, Standard Toolbar, 60

D

data, 2-3
        adding to charts, 108
        in cells
            aligning, 75-77
            clearing, 66-67
            editing, 56-57
            finding, 68-69
            replacing, 70
            sorting, 71-72
data markers, 109-110, 129
Data menu, Sort command, 71-72
data series, 111, 129

dates
> entering in cells, 46
> formats, 45
> in headers and footers, 97

Decrease Decimal button,
> Formatting Toolbar, 74

Delete command (Edit menu), 65

Delete Sheet command (Edit
> menu), 65

deleting
> chart elements, 112
> columns, 64-65
> embedded charts, 113
> macros, 121
> page breaks, 95
> rows, 64-65
> worksheets from
> > workbooks, 65

dialog boxes
> Auto Format, 82
> ChartWizard, 101, 106-108
> Column Width, 79
> components, 19
> > selecting, 20
> exiting without making
> > selections, 18-19
> Find, 68-69
> Find File, 34
> Format Cells
> > Alignment tab, 76-77
> > Font tab, 81
> > Number tab, 46, 73-74
> Function Wizard, 53-54
> Macro, 119-121, 123
> Macro Options, 123
> moving, 20
> Open, 27, 33
> Options, Edit tab, 60
> Page Setup, 91-92
> > Header/Footer tab,
> > > 96-98
> > Page tab, 86
> Paste Special, 108
> Print, 84-86, 88
> Record New Macro, 116-118
> Replace, 70
> Run, 126
> Save As, 31
> Search, 25, 34
> Setup, 127-128
> Sort, 71-72
> Toolbars, 22

directories, 10, 28, 129

disk drives, 8

disks, 8, 10

division (/) operator, 47

documents, *see* worksheets

dollar sign ($), absolute
> references, 59

double-clicking mouse, 9, 13, 129

doughnut charts, 105

Drag and Drop
> adding data to charts, 108
> enabling, 60

dragging with mouse, 20, 130

drop-down list boxes, 19
> selecting, 20

E

Edit menu commands
> Clear, 66
> Delete, 65
> Delete Sheet, 65
> Find, 68-69
> Replace, 70
> Undo, 65

editing, 2
> cell contents, 56-57
> charts, 107-108
> macros, 121

ellipsis (…), 17, 130

embedded charts, 106, 130
> deleting, 113

equals sign (=), entering
> formulas, 48

Esc (Escape) key, 8
> cancelling macros in
> > progress, 120
> exiting menus/dialog
> > boxes without making
> > selections, 18

Excel 5.0, 1
> exiting, 35
> installing, 125-128
> screen elements, 14-16
> starting, 12-13

Exit command (File menu), 35

exiting
> dialog boxes without making
> > selections, 19
> Excel 5.0, 35
> menus/dialog boxes without
> > making selections, 18

exponentiation (^) operator, 47

F

File menu commands
> Close, 30
> Exit, 35
> New, 29
> Open, 27-28, 33-34
> Page Setup, 92, 97-98
> Print, 84-85, 87-88
> Print Preview, 89-90
> Run (Program Manager), 126
> Save, 31
> Save As, 32

file names in headers and
> footers, 97

files, 9-10, 28, 130
> extensions, 32
> .XLS, 31

see also workbooks

Find command (Edit menu), 68-69

Find File button, Open dialog box,
> 33-34

finding data in cells, 68-69

floppy disks, 10

Font list, Formatting Toolbar, 82

Font Size list, Formatting
> Toolbar, 82

fonts, 80-82, 130
> in headers and footers, 97

footers, 91-92, 96-98

Format menu commands
> Auto Format, 82
> Cells
> > Alignment tab, 76-77
> > Font tab, 81
> > Number tab, 46, 73-74
> Column
> > AutoFit Selection, 78
> > Width, 79

formats
> cells, 67, 129
> charts, 101
> dates and times, 45
> numbers, 73-74

formatting, 2-3
> alignment, 75-77
> attributes, 80-82
> cell widths, 78-79
> fonts, 80-82
> headers and footers, 91-92,
> > 96-98
> margins, 90-92
> page breaks, 93-95
> page setups, 91-92

Formatting Toolbar, 14
    Bold style button, 82
    Comma style button, 74
    Currency style button, 74
    Decrease Decimal button, 74
    Font list, 82
    Font Size list, 82
    Increase Decimal button, 74
    Italic style button, 82
    Percent style button, 74
    Underline style button, 82
formula bar, 2, 41
    buttons, 57
formulas, 2-3
    averaging values, 49
    displaying, 41
    entering
        cell ranges, 50-51
        functions, 52-54
        in cells, 48
    operator precedence, 47
Function command (Insert menu),
    53-54
function keys, 8
Function Wizard button, Standard
    Toolbar, 54
functions, 49, 52, 131
    arguments, 129
    entering in cells, 53-54

G-H

grayed-out commands, 17, 130
gridlines, adding, 92

handles
    selection, 107
    sizing, 90
hard disks, 10
headers and footers, 91-92, 96-98
headings, 40
help, 24-26
    Toolbar/Toolbox button
        information, 22
Help button, Standard Toolbar, 26
Help menu, Contents command, 24
hiding TipWizard, 15
horizontal (landscape)
    orientation, 91
hot keys, 17, 130
How To window, 25

I

icons
    Microsoft Excel, 13
    program, 13, 131
    program group, 12-13, 130
    Program Manager, 126
Increase Decimal button,
    Formatting Toolbar, 74
Insert menu commands
    Chart As New Sheet, 106
    Columns, 63
    Function, 53-54
    Page Break, 95
    Remove Page Break, 95
    Rows, 63
    Worksheet, 63
insertion cursor, 56, 130
installing Excel, 125-128
Italic style button, Formatting
    Toolbar, 82
italic text, macro for, 118

J-K

jump terms, 24

keyboard shortcuts, *see* shortcut
    keys
keyboards, 7-8
keys
    alphanumeric, 8
    Alt (Alternative), 8
        with selection letters,
            18
    arrow, 8
    Ctrl (Control), 8
    Esc (Escape), 8
        cancelling macros in
            progress, 120
        exiting menus/dialog
            boxes without mak-
            ing selection, 18
    function, 8
    hot, 17, 130

L

labels, 40, 130
    alignment, 42
    changing values to, 42
    entering in cells, 41
landscape (horizontal)
    orientation, 91

leading zeros, 44
Left Align button, Standard
    Toolbar, 77
left-aligned data, 75
Legend button, Chart Toolbox, 111
legends, 101-102, 111, 130
line charts, 104-105
list boxes, 19
    selecting, 20

M

Macro command (Tools menu),
    119-123
Macro-name commands (Tools
    menu), 122-123
macros, 116
    assigning to menus, 122-123
    cancelling in-progress, 120
    deleting, 121
    editing, 121
    playing, 119-120
    recording, 116-118
manual page breaks, 94
margins, 90-92
mathematical calculations
    averaging, 49
    displaying results, 48
    functions, 52-54
    operator precedence, 47
Maximize button, 16
memory, RAM (random-access
    memory), 8
menu bar, 14
menus
    assigning macros to, 122-123
    exiting without making
        selections, 18
    selecting commands, 17-18
Microsoft Excel icon, 13
Minimize button, 16
minimized windows, 13, 130
monitors, 7
mouse, 7, 13
    clicking, 129
    double-clicking, 129
    dragging, 130
    operations, 9, 13
    pointing, 130
moving
    cells, 58-61
    dialog boxes, 20
multiplication (*) operator, 47

N

New command (File menu), 29
New Workbook button, Standard
    Toolbar, 29
numbering pages, 91
    in headers and footers, 97
numbers, *see* values

O

Open button, Standard Toolbar, 28
Open command (File menu), 27-28,
    33-34
opening workbooks, 27-28
operator precedence, 47, 49, 130
operators, 49, 130
option buttons, 19
    selecting, 20
Options command (Tools menu),
    Edit tab, 57, 60
orientation, 130
    data, 75
    worksheets, 91

P

Page Break command (Insert
    menu), 95
page breaks, 93-95, 130
Page Setup command (File menu),
    92, 97-98
Page Setup dialog box, 91-92
    Header/Footer tab, 96-98
    Page tab, 86
pages
    numbering, 91
        in headers and footers,
        97
    setting up, 91-92
paper size and quality, 91
Paste button, Standard Toolbar, 60
Paste Special dialog box, 108
Percent style button, Formatting
    Toolbar, 74
pie charts, 104-105
playing macros, 119-120
pointing mouse, 9, 13, 130
portrait (vertical) orientation, 91
ports, 8
pound signs (#), values in cells,
    78-79
precedence of operations, 47,
    49, 130

previewing worksheets, 89-90
print areas, 130
Print button, Standard Toolbar, 86
Print command (File menu), 84-85,
    87-88
Print Preview button, Standard
    Toolbar, 90
Print Preview command (File
    menu), 89-90
printers, selecting, 84
printing
    ranges, 87-88
    worksheets/workbooks, 85-86
program group icons, 12-13, 130
program groups, 13, 130
program icons, 13, 131
Program Manager icon, 126
programs, spreadsheet, 1

Q-R

quotes, single ('), changing values
    to labels, 42

RAM (random-access memory), 8
ranges, 38, 50-51, 129
    printing, 87-88
    selecting, 39
Record Macro command (Tools
    menu)
        Record New Macro, 117-118
        Stop Recording, 117-118
recording macros, 116-118
references
    absolute, 59
    cells, 3, 49, 129
    relative, 58-59
    sheets, 49
relative references, 58-59
Remove Page Break command
    (Insert menu), 95
Replace command (Edit menu), 70
replacing data in cells, 57, 70
Restore button, 16
Right Align button, Standard
    Toolbar, 77
right-aligned data, 75
right-clicking mouse, 9
rows, 2, 14, 131
    deleting, 64-65
    headings, 40
    inserting into worksheets,
        62-63
    selecting, 39, 62

Rows command (Insert menu), 63
Run command (Program Manager
    File menu), 126

S

Save As command (File menu), 32
Save button, Standard Toolbar, 32
Save command (File menu), 31
saving workbooks, 31-32
scaling worksheets, 91, 131
    to fit certain numbers of
        pages, 86
scatter charts, 104-105
screens, Excel 5.0 elements, 14-16
scroll arrows, 16
scroll bars, 14
scrolling windows, 16
search button (help), 24
searching for workbooks, 33-34
Select All button, 131
selecting
    cells, 38-39
    columns, 62
    dialog box components, 20
    menu commands, 17-18
    printers, 84
    rows, 62
    Toolbar buttons, 21
selection handles, 107
selection letters, 17, 131
Setup dialog boxes, 127-128
sheet references, 49
shortcut keys, 17
    Close (Ctrl+F4), 30
    Copy (Ctrl+C), 60
    Cut (Ctrl+X), 60
    Edit (F2), 56
    Exit (Alt+F4), 35
    Find (Ctrl+F), 68
    Format Cells (Ctrl+1), 73
    Help (F1), 24
    New (Ctrl+N), 29
    Open (Ctrl+O), 28
    Print (Ctrl+P), 84
    Replace (Ctrl+H), 70
    Save (Ctrl+S), 31
    Select Column
        (Ctrl+Spacebar), 62
    Select Row
        (Shift+Spacebar), 62
    Shortcut Menu
        (Shift+F10), 67

137

Index

shortcut menu commands
Clear Contents, 67
Delete, 65
Format Cells, 46
Insert, 63
single quote ('), changing values to
labels, 42
sizes of paper, 91
sizing handles, 90
Sort command (Data menu), 71-72
sorting cell data, 71-72
spreadsheet programs, 1
spreadsheets, 1
SQRT function, 49
Standard Toolbar, 14
Auto Sum button, 54
Center Across Columns
button, 77
Center Align button, 77
ChartWizard button, 100
Copy button, 60
Cut button, 60
Function Wizard button, 54
Help button, 26
Left Align button, 77
New Workbook button, 29
Open button, 28
Paste button, 60
Print button, 86
Print Preview button, 90
Right Align button, 77
Save button, 32
TipWizard button, 15
Undo button, 65
starting Excel 5.0, 12-13
status bar, 14, 56, 131
stepping through macros, 119
Stop Macro button, Macro Toolbox,
117-118
Stop Recording command (Tools
Record Macro submenu), 117
stopping macros in progress, 120
styles, text, 80-82, 131
subdirectories, 10
subtraction (–) operator, 47
SUM function, 49
system units, 7-8

T

tab scrolling buttons, 2, 14
tabs, 2
dialog boxes, 19
selecting, 20
worksheet, 14

text, 2-3
attached, 129
attributes, 80-82
changing values to, 42
charts
labels, 102
legends, 101-102, 111
titles, 101
labels, 40
overrunning cells, 78-79
unattached, 131
text boxes, 19
selecting, 20
text styles, 80-82, 131
times
entering in cells, 46
formats, 45
in headers and footers, 97
TipWizard, 15
title bar, 14, 16, 19
titles, 40
charts, 101
toggles, 20, 131
Toolbars, 21, 23, 131
changing into Toolboxes, 23
displaying, 22
Formatting, see Formatting
Toolbar
selecting buttons, 21
Standard, see Standard
Toolbar
Toolbars command (View
menu), 22
Toolboxes, 21, 23, 131
changing into Toolbars, 23
Chart, 104-105, 107, 111
displaying, 22
Macro, 117-118
Tools menu commands
Macro, 119-123
Macro-name, 122-123
Options, Edit tab, 57, 60
Record Macro
Record New Macro,
117-118
Stop Recording, 117
ToolTips, 22

U-V

unattached text, 131
Underline style button, Formatting
Toolbar, 82
Undo button, Standard Toolbar, 65

Undo command (Edit menu), 65
undoing
deleted rows/columns, 65
deleted embedded
charts, 113
values, 2-3, 43
alignment, 42
averaging, 49
changing
in charts for what-if
analysis, 109-110
to labels, 42
dates and times, 45-46
entering in cells, 44
formats, changing, 73-74
vertical (portrait) orientation, 91
View menu, Toolbars command, 22

W

what-if analysis, changing values in
charts, 109-110
Width command (Format Column
submenu), 79
WIN command, 12, 126
windows
chart, 106
closing, 16
How To, 25
minimized, 13, 130
minimizing, maximizing, and
restoring, 16
scrolling, 16
workbooks, 2-3, 131
closing, 30
copying/moving data
between, 60
creating, 29
deleting worksheets, 65
features, 1-2
inserting worksheets, 63
opening, 27-28
printing, 85-86
saving, 31-32
searching for, 33-34
Worksheet command (Insert
menu), 63
worksheet functions, 131
worksheet tabs, 14
worksheets, 2, 14
active, 14
chart, 106
copying/moving data
between, 60

deleting
    columns/rows, 64-65
    embedded charts, 113
    from workbooks, 65
features, 1-2
gridlines, adding, 92
inserting
    columns/rows, 62-63
    into workbooks, 63
previewing, 89-90
printing, 85-86
scaling, 131
    to fit certain numbers
      of pages, 86
selecting, 39
zooming, 89

X-Z

.XLS file extension, 31

zeros, leading, 44
zooming worksheets, 89